Israel in Egypt

in Full Score

George Frideric
HANDEL

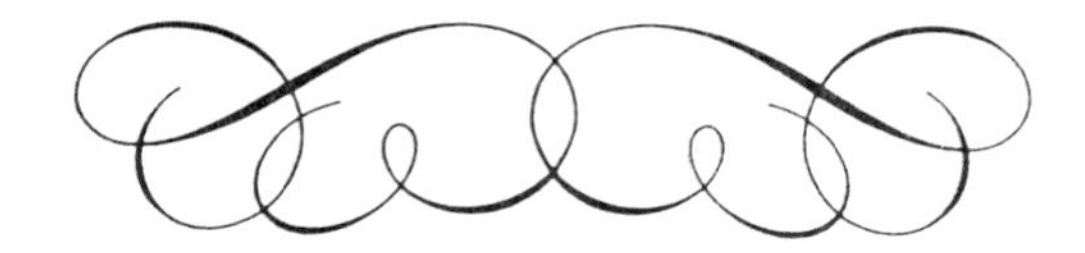

DOVER PUBLICATIONS, INC.
Mineola, New York

Published in Canada by General Publishing Company, Ltd., 30 Lesmill Road, Don Mills, Toronto, Ontario.
Published in the United Kingdom by Constable and Company, Ltd., 3 The Lanchesters, 162–164 Fulham Palace Road, London W6 9ER.

Bibliographical Note

This Dover publication, first published in 1998, is a complete and unabridged republication of *Israel in Egypt / An Oratorio by George Frederic Handel,* edited by Friedrich Chrysander and issued as Part XVI *of The Works of G. F. Handel, printed for The German Handel Society by Breitkopf & Härtel,* 1863. The instrumentation list is newly added.

International Standard Book Number: 0-486-40411-0

Manufactured in the United States of America
Dover Publications, Inc., 31 East 2nd Street, Mineola, N.Y. 11501

PREFACE.

Of the Oratorio Israel in Egypt the last part was composed first, from the 1st to the 11th October 1738; then the preceeding part, from the 15th to the 28th of the same month; the work was complete as a whole on the 1st November. But the present first part was Handel's second; and the Anthem on the death of Queen Caroline was converted into a first part under the designation »*The lamentation of the Israelites for the death of Joseph*«. Handel himself compiled the text this time, from Psalms 78, 105 and 106; the second part being formed by the Song of the Israelites on the Red Sea in Exodus 15. The titles, which we here give for the first time, likewise have Handel for their author. The first performance took place on the 4th April 1739. All further information on the composition and the remarkable vicissitudes of this great work will shortly be found in the 3d vol. of my Life of Handel.

In consequence of the few performances, the score remained almost absolutely in its original condition, or at least suffered no alterations which would have to be regarded in a new edition. The solitary exception is found at the end of the chorus »Who is like unto Thee?« Here in the original, at the words »*doing wonders*«, Handel put a 𝄐 over the last *E* in the *continuo* (p. 216, bar 1), and in the conducting score drew his pencil through the three following bars »*Thou stretchest out thy right hand*«, and curiously at the same time wrote the following bass under them:

exactly as here printed. A later copy taken by Smith, doubtless not till after Handel's death, suppresses the cancelled bars and winds up in *E* major with »*doing wonders*«, and thus leaves us completely in the dark about the enigmatical addition. This omission of the three bars certainly rests on a misconception; for Handel doubtless only cancelled them in the year 1746, when, on employing the movement for the so-called Occasional Oratorio, he could make no use of these three last bars leading to the following chorus. On the same occasion he also probably sketched the bass just quoted, and was only prevented from filling in the other parts by the interval of ten years which elapsed before the next performance, and by the many curtailments which were then required. This filling in I myself have now supplied, inserting the four bars in question in the score, but with smaller notes, that my additions may be at once distinguishable. By the repetition of the words »*fearful of praises, doing wonders!*« a better wind-up may perhaps be attained, and the monotony in the modulation be avoided, which existed between the former ending and the following »*Thou stretchest out thy right hand*«.

But an addition of unquestionably and incomparably more importance has been given to the present edition, in the accompaniment of three trombones, which — incredible as it may seem after the many editions of Israel — is here for the first time made public. This trombone accompaniment is not found in the original, but only in the conducting score in an appendix. Thus it must (like that to Saul) have been noted down by Handel separately from the score, and might the more easily be lost. May this important contribution cause the later so-called enrichments of the score to appear superfluous, and bring them more and more into discredit.

The edition of Israel for the former London Handel Society was undertaken by *Mendelssohn*, who furnished it with an organ accompaniment. Such an addition might certainly be highly acceptable; but Mendelssohn's is unfortunately conceived throughout in a manner not perfectly in accordance with Handel's own (as will be further discussed in vol. 2 of the »Jahrbücher für musikalische Wissenschaft«).

The pianoforte accompaniments are always by the editor when no other name is mentioned.

Leipzig, August 1, 1863.

Chr.

ISRAEL IN EGYPT.
Israel in Aegypten.

PARTE PRIMA.

EXODUS.

Page

RECITATIVE. (Tenore.)

Now there arose a new king over Egypt, which knew not Joseph; and he set over Israel task-masters to afflict them with burdens; and they made them serve with rigour 1

CHORUS.

And the children of Israel sighed by reason of the bondage: And their cry came up unto God. They oppress'd them with burdens, and made them serve with rigour 1

RECITATIVE.

Then sent He Moses, His servant, and Aaron, whom He had chosen: these shew'd His signs among them, and wonders in the land of Ham. — He turned their waters into blood 17

CHORUS.

They loathed to drink of the river: He turned their waters into blood 17

AIR. (Alto.)

Their land brought forth frogs, yea, even in the King's chambers. He gave their cattle over to the pestilence; blotches and blains broke forth on man and beast. 23

CHORUS.

He spake the word: And there came all manner of flies and lice in all their quarters 27

He spake: and the locusts came without number and devour'd the fruits of the land 37

CHORUS.

He gave them hailstones for rain; fire, mingled with the hail, ran along upon the ground 41

CHORUS.

He sent a thick darkness over all the land, even darkness, which might be felt 55

CHORUS.

He smote all the first-born of Egypt, the chief of all their strength. 58

CHORUS.

But as for His people, He led them forth like sheep. He brought them out with silver and gold: there was not one feeble person among their tribes. 72

CHORUS.

Egypt was glad when they departed, for the fear of them fell upon them 82

DER AUSZUG.

Seite

RECITATIV. (Tenor.)

Nun kam ein neuer König in Aegypten, dem Joseph fremd war; und er setzt' über Israel Frohnvögte, die sie drückten mit Arbeit, und mit Diensten unbarmherzig . 1

CHOR.

Und die Kinder Israel schrien in ihrer harten Knechtschaft: Und ihr Schrein stieg auf zu dem Herrn. Sie erlagen der Arbeit und weinten laut um Rettung . . 1

RECITATIV.

Da sandt' Er Moses, Seinen Diener, und Aaron, den Er erwählet: die wirkten Seine Zeichen und Wunder in dem Lande Ham. — Des Stromes Gewässer ward zu Blut 17

CHOR.

Mit Ekel erfüllte der Trank nun: des Stromes Gewässer ward zu Blut 17

ARIE. (Alt.)

Der Strom zeugte Frösche, die füllten das Land, ja, kamen in des Königs Kammer. Er liess von Seuchen schlagen alle Heerdentrift; schwarzes Geschwür brach aus an Mensch und Thier 23

CHOR.

Er sprach das Wort: Und es kam der Fliegen Gewühl, der Fliegen und Mücken Schwarm in ihre Höfe. 27

Er sprach: und der Zug der Heuschrecken kam und tilgte alle Frucht auf dem Feld 37

CHOR.

Er sandte Hagel herab, Feu'r in dem Hagelsturm rauscht im Donner auf das Land 41

CHOR.

Er sandte dicke Finsterniss über all das Land, tiefes Nachtgrau'n, dass niemand sah. 55

CHOR.

Er schlug alle Erstgeburt Aegypten's, den Kern der ganzen Macht. 58

CHOR.

Doch mit dem Volk Israel zog er dahin gleichwie ein Hirt. Er führt' es hinaus mit Silber und Gold: führte das ganze Heer aus Aegypten auf Einen Tag. . 72

CHOR.

Froh sah Aegypten seinen Auszug, denn die Furcht vor ihm überkam sie 82

CHORUS.

Page

He rebuked the Red Sea, and it was dried up . . 93
He led them through the deep as through a wilderness. 95
But the waters overwhelmed their enemies, there was not one of them left 105

CHORUS.

And Israel saw that great work that the Lord did upon th' Egyptians; and the people feared the Lord. . 109
And believed the Lord and his servant Moses. . . 111

CHOR.

Seite

Er gebot der Meerflut: und sie trocknete aus. . . 93
Er führte durch die Tiefe trocken sie hindurch wie durch ein Wüstenland 95
Doch die Feinde überströmte die Wasserflut, dass auch nicht Einer entkam 105

CHOR.

Und Israel sah dieses Werk, das der Herr that am Land Aegypten; und ganz Israel fürchtete ihn . . 109
Und erkannte den Herrn und seinen Diener Moses 111

PARTE SECONDA.

MOSES' SONG.

INTROITUS. (Chorus.)

Page

Moses, and the children of Israel sung this song unto the Lord, and spake, saying: 115

CHORUS.

I will sing unto the Lord, for he hath triumphed gloriously, the horse and his rider hath he thrown into the sea. 119

DUET. (Soprano I. II.)

The Lord is my strength and my song, He is become my salvation. 138

CHORUS.

He is my God, and I will prepare him an habitation: my father's God. 143
And I will exalt him. 145

DUET. (Basso I. II.)

The Lord is a man of war, Lord is his name; Pharaoh's chariots, and his host, hath he cast into the sea. His chosen captains also are drowned in the Red Sea. . 153

CHORUS.

The depths have covered them, they sank into the bottom as a stone 169

CHORUS.

Thy right hand, oh Lord, is become glorious in power: thy right hand, oh Lord, hath dashed in pieces the enemy 173
And in the greatness of thine excellency, thou hast overthrown them that rose up against thee. 183
Thou sentest forth thy wrath, which consumed them as stubble 185

CHORUS.

And with the blast of thy nostrils the waters were gathered together, the floods stood upright as an heap, the depths were congealed in the heart of the sea . . . 195

AIR. (Tenore.)

The enemy said: I will pursue, I will overtake, I will divide the spoil: my lust shall be satisfied upon them: I will draw my sword: my hand shall destroy them 205

MOSES' GESANG.

INTROITUS. (Chor.)

Seite

Moses und die Kinder von Israel sangen also zu dem Herrn, ihn laut preisend: 115

CHOR.

Ich will singen zu dem Herrn, denn er hat geholfen wunderbar, das Ross und den Reiter hat gestürzt er in das Meer 119

DUETT. (Sopran I. II.)

Der Herr ist mein Heil und mein Lied, Er ward allein mein Erlöser 138

CHOR.

Er ist mein Gott, und ich will bereiten ihm eine Wohnung: meines Vaters Gott. 143
Und ich will ihn preisen 145

DUETT. (Bass I. II.)

Der Herr ist der starke Held, Herr ist sein Nam'; Pharao's Wagen und sein Heer hat er in das Meer gestürzt. All' seine Helden, alle versanken in dem Schilfmeer 153

CHOR.

Die Tiefe deckte sie, sie sanken in den Abgrund wie ein Stein 169

CHOR.

O Herr, deine Hand thut grosse herrliche Wunder: dein Arm hat, o Herr, zerschlagen in Stücke die Feindesmacht. 173
Und in der Grösse deiner Herrlichkeit hast du sie gestürzt all' die gegen dich stritten 183
Du sandtest deinen Grimm, der verzehrte sie wie Stoppeln 185

CHOR.

Und vor dem Hauch deines Mundes zertheilten sich alsobald die Wasser, die Flut stand aufrecht wie ein Wall, die Tiefe erstarrte im Herzen der See. 195

ARIE. (Tenor.)

So sagte der Feind: ich eile nach, bis ich sie erhascht, bis ich getheilet den Raub, und stille die Rachelust an ihnen; ich will zieh'n mein Schwert, mein Arm soll sie verderben 205

AIR. (Soprano.)

Page

Thou didst blow with the wind: the sea cover'd them, they sank as lead in the mighty waters 210

CHORUS.

Who is like unto Thee, oh Lord, among the Gods? who is like Thee, glorious in holiness, fearful in praises, doing wonders! Thou stretchest out thy right hand: . 214

The earth swallowed them 217

DUET. (Alto. Tenore.)

Thou in thy mercy hast led forth thy people which thou hast redeemed. Thou hast guided them in thy strength unto thy holy habitation 221

CHORUS.

The people shall hear and be afraid: sorrow shall take hold on them; all th' inhabitants of Canaan shall melt away by the greatness of thy arm. They shall be as still as a stone, till thy people pass over, oh Lord, till thy people pass over, which thou hast purchased . . . 226

AIR. (Alto.)

Thou shalt bring them in, and plant them in the mountain of thine inheritance, in the place, oh Lord, which thou hast made for thee to dwell in, in the sanctuary, oh Lord, which thy hands have established . 250

CHORUS.

The Lord shall reign for ever and ever 254

RECITATIVE.

For the horse of Pharaoh went in with his chariots and with his horsemen into the sea, and the Lord brought again the waters of the sea upon them: but the children of Israel went on dry land in the midst of the sea . . . 257

CHORUS.

The Lord shall reign for ever and ever.
(ut supra p. 254.)

RECITATIVE.

And Miriam the prophetess, the sister of Aaron, took a timbrel in her hand, and all the women went out after her with timbrels and with dances, and Miriam answered them: 257

CHORUS.
Soprano, solo.

Sing ye to the Lord, for he hath triumphed gloriously! 258

Tutti.

The Lord shall reign for ever and ever 258

Soprano, solo.

The horse and his rider hath he thrown into the sea 259

Tutti.

The Lord shall reign for ever and ever: I will sing unto the Lord, for he hath triumphed gloriously, the horse and his rider hath he thrown into the sea . . . 260

ARIE. (Sopran.)

Seite

Aber du liessest weh'n deinen Hauch: das Meer deckte sie, sie sanken wie Blei in dem mächt'gen Wasser 210

CHOR.

Wer vergleichet sich Dir, o Herr, unter den Göttern? wer gleichet Dir, glanzvoll in Heiligkeit, schrecklich und herrlich, wunderthätig! Du strecktest aus die Rechte: 214

Da verschlang sie das Grab 217

DUETT. (Alt. Tenor.)

Du in deiner Gnade hast dein Volk geleitet, das du hast erlöset. Und du hast geführt sie mit Macht zu deiner heiligen Wohnung 221

CHOR.

Das hören die Völker und sind erstaunt: Schrecken fasst sie rings umher; all' die Eingebornen Kanaan's ergreift die Angst durch die Stärke deines Arms. Sie werden erstarren wie Stein, bis vorüber dein Volk zieht, o Herr, bis vorüber dein Volk zieht, das du erworben hast. 226

ARIE. (Alt.)

Bringe sie hinein, und pflanze sie auf den Bergen in deinem Erbtheil, an den Ort, o Herr, den du erhoh't zu deiner Wohnung und zu deinem Heiligthum, o Herr, das deine Hand hat bereitet 250

CHOR.

Der Herr regiert auf immer und ewig! 254

RECITATIV.

Denn die Reiter Pharao's mit all ihren Wagen und ihren Rossen sanken in's Meer, und der Herr liess des Meer's gewalt'ge Fluten auf sie fallen: doch die Kinder von Israel gingen hindurch in der Mitte des Meer's . . 257

CHOR.

Der Herr regiert auf immer und ewig!
(*ut supra p.* 254.)

RECITATIV.

Und Mirjam die Seherin, die Schwester des Aaron, nahm die Pauk' in ihre Hand; die Schaar der Weiber sie folgte ihr nach mit Pauken und mit Reigen, und Mirjam sang vor ihr: 257

CHOR.
Sopran, solo.

Singet zu dem Herrn, denn er hat gesieget wunderbar! 258

Tutti.

Der Herr regiert auf immer und ewig! 258

Sopran, solo.

Das Ross und den Reiter hat er in das Meer gestürzt 259

Tutti.

Der Herr regiert auf immer und ewig: ich will singen zu dem Herrn, denn er hat geholfen wunderbar, das Ross und den Reiter hat gestürzt er in das Meer . 260

Israel in Egypt

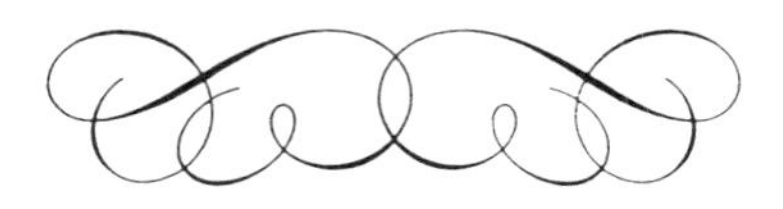

INSTRUMENTATION

2 Oboes
2 Bassoons [Fagotti]

2 Trumpets in C [Tromba]
3 Trombones*

Timpani

Violins I, II [Violino]
Violas
Cellos [Violoncelli]
Basses [Bassi]

Continuo* ["Tutti Bassi, e Cembalo"]
Organ* [Organo]

Pianoforte*

Vocal Soli:
Sopranos I, II, Alto, Tenor, Basses I, II

Double Chorus of Mixed Voices:
SSAATTBB

*For a detailed discussion of Handel's orchestra, and especially of continuo practice in the oratorio—including use of the positive organ and harpsichord—see Paul Henry Lang's *George Frideric Handel,* Chapter XXVI (Dover, 1996: 0-486-29227-4).

Friedrich Chrysander ["Chr."]—founder of the Handel-Gesellschaft and editor of this volume—added the pianoforte part in the form of a keyboard reduction and realization. For mention of this, Mendelssohn's organ accompaniment, and the inclusion of three trombones in this edition, see his preface, p. iii.

EXODUS.
DER AUSZUG.

Oboe I.
Oboe II.
Fagotti.
Violino I.
Violino II.
Viola.
SOPRANO I.
(Tutti.)
And their cry came up un-to God.
Und ihr Schreïn stieg auf zu dem Herrn.
ALTO I.
And their cry came up un-to God.
Und ihr Schreïn stieg auf zu dem Herrn.
TENORE I.
BASSO I.
SOPRANO II.
And their cry came up un-to God.
Und ihr Schreïn stieg auf zu dem Herrn.
ALTO II.
And their cry came up un-to God.
Und ihr Schreïn stieg auf zu dem Herrn.
TENORE II.
BASSO II.
Tutti Bassi.
Organo.
mf

They oppress'd them with burdens, and made them serve with ri - gour, with
Sie er - la - gen der Ar - beit und wein - ten laut um Ret - tung, um
They oppress'd them with burdens, and made them
Sie er - la - gen der Ar - beit und wein - ten
They oppress'd them with burdens, and made them serve, and made them serve with
Sie er - la - gen der Ar - beit und wein - ten laut, und wein - ten laut um
They oppress'd them with burdens, and made them serve with ri - gour, with
Sie er - la - gen der Ar - beit und wein - ten laut um Ret - tung, um
They oppress'd them with burdens, and made them
Sie er - la - gen der Ar - beit und wein - ten
They oppress'd them with burdens, and made them serve, and made them serve with
Sie er - la - gen der Ar - beit und wein - ten laut, und wein - ten laut um

ri - gour; they op-press'd them with burdens, and made them serve,
Ret - tung; sie er - la - gen der Ar-beit und wein - ten laut,
serve, and made them serve with ri - gour;
laut, und wein - ten laut um Ret - tung;
ri-gour, and made them serve, and made them serve with
Ret-tung, und wein - ten laut, und wein - - - - ten laut um
And their cry came up un - to
Und ihr Schreïn stieg auf zu dem
ri - gour; they op-press'd them with burdens, and made them serve,
Ret - tung; sie er - la - gen der Ar-beit und wein - ten laut,
serve, and made them serve with ri - gour;
laut, und wein - ten laut um Ret - tung;
ri-gour, and made them serve, and made them serve with
Ret-tung, und wein - ten laut, und wein - - - - ten laut um
And their cry came up un - to
Und ihr Schreïn stieg auf zu dem

they oppress'd them with
sie er-la-gen der
they oppress'd them with burdens, and made them serve, they oppress'd them with burdens, and made them
sie er-la-gen der Ar-beit und wein-ten laut, sie er-la-gen der Ar-beit und wein-ten
ri-gour; and their cry came
Ret-tung; und ihr Schreïn stieg
God, and their cry came
Herrn, und ihr Schreïn stieg
they oppress'd them with burdens, and made them
sie er-la-gen der Ar-beit und wein-ten
they oppress'd them with burdens, and made them serve; and their cry came
sie er-la-gen der Ar-beit und wein-ten laut; und ihr Schreïn stieg
ri-gour; and their cry came
Ret-tung; und ihr Schreïn stieg
God, and their cry came
Herrn, und ihr Schreïn stieg

burdens, and made them serve, and made them serve with ri - gour, and they made them
Ar-beit und wein-ten laut, und wein-ten laut um Ret - tung, und sie wein-ten
serve, and they made them serve with ri - gour;
laut, und sie wein-ten laut um Ret - tung;
up un-to God;
auf zu dem Herrn;
up un-to God; they oppress'd them with burdens, and made them serve with
auf zu dem Herrn; sie er-la-gen der Ar-beit und wein-ten laut um
serve, and made them serve, and made them serve with ri - gour, and they made them
laut, und wein-ten laut, und wein-ten laut um Ret - tung, und sie wein-ten
up un-to God, their cry came up un-to God,
auf zu dem Herrn, ihr Schreïn stieg auf zu dem Herrn,
up un-to God; they oppress'd them with burdens,
auf zu dem Herrn; sie er-la-gen der Ar-beit,
up un-to God; they oppress'd them with burdens, and made them serve with
auf zu dem Herrn; sie er-la-gen der Ar-beit und wein-ten laut um

serve; and their cry came up un-to God;
laut; und ihr Schrein stieg auf zu dem Herrn;
and their cry came up un-to God,
und ihr Schrein stieg auf zu dem Herrn,
and they made them serve, and their cry
und sie wein-ten laut, und ihr Schrein
ri-gour, they made them serve with
Ret-tung, sie wein-ten laut um
serve; and their cry came up un-to God;
laut; und ihr Schrein stieg auf zu dem Herrn;
and they made them serve, and their cry
und sie wein-ten laut, und ihr Schrein
they oppress'd them with burdens, and made them serve with
sie er-la-gen der Ar-beit und wein-ten laut um
ri-gour, they oppress'd them with burdens, and made them serve with
Ret-tung, sie er-la-gen der Ar-beit und wein-ten laut um

they oppress'd them with burdens, and made them serve with ri - gour,
sie er-la-gen der Ar-beit und wein-ten laut um Ret - tung,
came up, came up un - - - to
stieg auf, stieg auf zu dem
came up, came up
stieg auf, stieg auf
ri - - gour; they oppress'd them with
Ret - - tung; sie er-la-gen der
they oppress'd them with burdens, and made them serve with ri - gour,
sie er-la-gen der Ar-beit und wein-ten laut um Ret - tung,
came up, came up
stieg auf, stieg auf
ri - - gour, and they made them serve
Ret - - tung, und sie wein-ten laut
ri - - gour, and they made them serve
Ret - - tung, und sie wein-ten laut

and they made them serve with ri - gour, with ri - - - - gour.
und sie wein-ten laut um Ret - tung, um Ret - - - - tung.
God, and they made them serve with ri - gour.
Herrn, und sie wein-ten laut um Ret - tung.
un - to God, and they made them serve with ri - gour.
zu dem Herrn, und sie wein-ten laut um Ret - tung.
burdens, and made them serve with ri - gour, with ri - gour. And the child-ren of
Ar-beit und wein-ten laut um Ret - tung, um Ret - tung. Und die Kin - der
and they made them serve with ri - gour, with ri - - - - gour.
und sie wein-ten laut um Ret - tung, um Ret - - - - tung.
un - to God, and they made them serve with ri - gour.
zu dem Herrn, und sie wein-ten laut um Ret - tung.
with ri - - - - - - - - gour, and made them serve with ri - gour.
um Ret - - - - - - - - tung, und wein-ten laut um Ret - tung.
with ri - - - - - - gour, with ri - - gour. And the child-ren of
um Ret - - - - - - tung, um Ret - - tung. Und die Kin - der

And the children of Is-ra-el sigh'd by rea-son
Und die Kin-der Is-ra-el schrien in ih-rer
And the child-ren of Is-ra-el sigh'd, sigh'd, sigh'd, sigh'd by rea-son
Und die Kin-der Is-ra-el schrien, schrien, schrien, schrien in ih-rer
And the child-ren of Is-ra-el sigh'd, sigh'd by rea-son
Und die Kin-der Is-ra-el schrien, schrien in ih-rer
Is-ra-el sigh'd, sigh'd, sigh'd, sigh'd, sigh'd, sigh'd by rea-son
Is-ra-el schrien, schrien, schrien, schrien, schrien, schrien in ih-rer
And the child-ren of Is-ra-el sigh'd, the children of Is-ra-el sigh'd by rea-son
Und die Kin-der Is-ra-el schrien, die Kin-der Is-ra-el schrien in ih-rer
And the children of Is-ra-el sigh'd by rea-son
Und die Kin-der Is-ra-el schrien in ih-rer
And the children of Is-ra-el sigh'd by rea-son
Und die Kin-der Is-ra-el schrien in ih-rer
Is-ra-el sigh'd, sigh'd, sigh'd, sigh'd, sigh'd, sigh'd by rea-son
Is-ra-el schrien, schrien, schrien, schrien, schrien, schrien in ih-rer

of the bon - dage; they oppress'd them with burdens, and made them serve,
har - ten Knechtschaft; sie er - la - gen der Ar - beit und wein - ten laut,
of the bon - dage; they oppress'd them with burdens, and made them
har - ten Knechtschaft; sie er - la - gen der Ar - beit und wein - ten
of the bon - dage; they oppress'd them with
har - ten Knechtschaft; sie er - la - gen der
of the bon - dage;
har - ten Knechtschaft;
of the bon - dage, they sigh'd, sigh'd, sigh'd;
har - ten Knechtschaft, sie schrien, schrien, schrien;
of the bon - dage, they sigh'd, sigh'd, sigh'd;
har - ten Knechtschaft, sie schrien, schrien, schrien;
of the bon - dage, they sigh'd, sigh'd, sigh'd,
har - ten Knechtschaft, sie schrien, schrien, schrien,
of the bon - dage, they sigh'd, sigh'd, sigh'd,
har - ten Knechtschaft, sie schrien, schrien, schrien,

they oppress'd them with
sie er-la-gen der
bur-dens, and made them
Ar-beit und wein-ten
serve, and they made them
laut, und sie wein-ten
serve,
laut,
serve, and made them
laut, und wein-ten
serve, they oppress'd them with
laut, sie er-la-gen der
bur-dens, and made them
Ar-beit und wein-ten
serve,
laut,
burdens, and made them
Ar-beit und wein-ten
serve,
laut,
and made them
und wein-ten
serve, they oppress'd them with
laut, sie er-la-gen der
and their
und ihr
cry
Schreïn
came
stieg
they oppress'd them with
sie er-la-gen der
bur-dens, and made them
Ar-beit und wein-ten
serve,
laut,
they oppress'd them with
sie er-la-gen der
bur-dens, and made them
Ar-beit und wein-ten
serve,
laut,
and their
und ihr
cry
Schreïn
came
stieg
and their
und ihr
cry
Schreïn
came
stieg

they oppress'd them with
sie er-la-gen der
burdens, and made them
Ar-beit und wein-ten
serve,
laut,
they oppress'd them with
sie er-la-gen der
burdens, and made them
Ar-beit und wein-ten
serve,
laut,
up,
auf,
came
stieg
up
auf
un - - - - - to
zu dem

burdens, and made them serve with ri - gour, with ri - gour,
Ar-beit und wein - ten laut um Ret - tung, um Ret - tung,
serve with
laut um
serve, and their cry came up un - to
laut, und ihr Schrei'n stieg auf zu dem
God; they oppress'd them with burdens, and made them serve, and made them
Herrn; sie er-la-gen der Ar-beit und wein - ten laut, und wein - ten
burdens, and made them serve with ri - gour, with ri - gour,
Ar-beit und wein - ten laut um Ret - tung, um Ret - tung,
serve, and their cry came up un - to
laut, und ihr Schrei'n stieg auf zu dem
God, came up un - to
Herrn, stieg auf zu dem
God; they oppress'd them with burdens, and made them serve, and made them
Herrn; sie er-la-gen der Ar-beit und wein - ten laut, und wein - ten

and they made them serve, and they made them serve, they made them serve with ri -
und sie wein-ten laut, und sie wein-ten laut, sie wein-ten laut um Ret -
ri - gour, and they made them serve, and they made them serve with ri -
Ret - tung, und sie wein-ten laut, und sie wein-ten laut um Ret -
God; and they made them serve, and they made them serve with ri -
Herrn; und sie wein-ten laut, und sie wein-ten laut um Ret -
serve, and they made them serve, and they made them serve with ri -
laut, und sie wein-ten laut, und sie wein-ten laut um Ret -
and they made them serve, and they made them serve, they made them serve with ri -
und sie wein-ten laut, und sie wein-ten laut, sie wein-ten laut um Ret -
God; and they made them serve, and they made them serve with ri -
Herrn; und sie wein-ten laut, und sie wein-ten laut um Ret -
God; and they made them serve, and they made them serve with ri -
Herrn; und sie wein-ten laut, und sie wein-ten laut um Ret -
serve, and they made them serve, and they made them serve with ri -
laut, und sie wein-ten laut, und sie wein-ten laut um Ret -
6
7 6

gour:
tung:
and their cry came up, came up unto God.
und ihr Schrei'n stieg auf, stieg auf zu dem Herrn.
gour:
tung:
and their cry came up, came up un-to God.
und ihr Schrei'n stieg auf, stieg auf zu dem Herrn.
gour:
tung:
and their cry came up, came up un - to God.
und ihr Schrei'n stieg auf, stieg auf zu dem Herrn.
gour:
tung:
and their cry came up, came up un - to God.
und ihr Schrei'n stieg auf, stieg auf zu dem Herrn.

Recitativo.
TENORE.
Continuo.
Then sent He Mo - ses, His servant, and Aa-ron, whom He had cho-sen: these shew'd His signs a - mong them, and wonders in the land of Ham. He turned their Wa-ters in - to blood.
Da sandt' Er Mo-ses, Sei-nen Die-ner, und Aa-ron, den Er er - wäh-let: die wirk - ten Sei - ne Zei-chen und Wunder in dem Lan-de Ham. Des Stromes Ge - wäs-ser ward zu Blut.
mf

CHORUS.
Largo assai.
senza Oboi.
Violino I.
Violino II.
Viola.
SOPRANO.
ALTO.
TENORE.
BASSO.
Tutti Bassi.
Tasto solo.
They loathed to
Mit E - kel er -
They loath-ed to drink of the ri - ver: He turn - ed their wa - - - - - -
Mit E - kel er - füll - te der Trank nun: des Stro - mes Ge - wäs - - - - - -
Largo, non adagio.
Pianoforte.
mf

They loath - ed to drink of the ri -
Mit E - kel er - füll - te der Trank
drink of the ri - ver: He turn - ed their wa -
füll - te der Trank nun: des Stro - mes Ge - wäs -
ters in - to blood, in - to blood; they
ser ward zu Blut, ward zu Blut; mit
ver: He turn - ed their wa - ters in - to blood;
nun: des Stro - mes Ge - wäs - ser ward zu Blut;
ters in - to blood; they loath - ed, they loath -
ser ward zu Blut; mit E - kel, mit E -
loath - ed to drink of the ri - ver, they loath -
E - kel er - füll - te der Trank nun, mit E -
They loath - ed to drink of the ri -
Mit E - kel er - füll - te der Trank

they loath - ed to drink of the ri - - - ver, they
mit E - kel er - füll - te der Trank nun, mit
- - ed to drink of the ri - ver, they loath - ed to
- - kel er - füll - te der Trank nun, mit E - kel der
- - ed to drink of the ri - ver,
- - kel er - füll - te der Trank nun,
ver: He turn - ed their wa - - - ters in - to
nun: des Stro - mes Ge - wäs - - - ser ward zu
loath - ed, they loath - ed to drink of the ri - ver: He turn - ed their
E - kel, mit E - kel er - füll - te der Trank nun: des Stro - mes Ge -
drink, they loath - - - ed to drink of the ri - ver: He turn - ed, He
Trank, mit E - - - kel er - füll - te der Trank nun: des Stro - mes Ge -
they loath - ed to drink of the ri -
mit E - kel er - füll - te der Trank
blood, in - to blood;
Blut, ward zu Blut;

wa - - - - - - ters in - to blood, their wa - - - - - - - - - - ters in - to
wäs - - - - - - ser ward zu Blut, Ge - wäs - - - - - - - - - ser ward zu
turn - ed their wa - ters, their wa - ters in - to blood, He turn - ed their wa - ters in - to
wäs - ser, des Stro - mes Ge - wäs - ser ward zu Blut, des Stro - mes Ge - wäs - ser ward zu
ver: He turn - ed their wa - ters in - to blood, He turn - ed their wa - ters in - to
nun: des Stro - mes Ge - wäs - ser ward zu Blut, des Stro - mes Ge - wäs - ser ward zu
6 7 7 6♭ 4 ♮ 7 8 6 4 5 ♮ 6 5 6 5 9 8 9 7 8 6 7 5
blood; they loathed to drink of the ri - - ver, they loath - - - - - - - - - - -
Blut; mit E - kel er - füll - te der Trank nun, mit E - - - - - - - - - - -
blood; they loath - ed to drink of the ri - ver, they loath - - ed to drink, they
Blut; mit E - kel er - füll - te der Trank nun, mit E - - kel der Trank, mit
blood; they loathed to drink of the ri - ver, they loath - - - - - - ed to
Blut; mit E - kel er - füll - te der Trank nun, mit E - - - - - - kel er -
they loathed to drink of the ri - ver, of the ri - - - ver, they loathed to
mit E - kel er - füll - te der Trank nun, er - füll - - te mit E - kel der
7 6♭ 6 5 7 6 6 5 7 6♭ 6 5♭ 6 6

ed, they loath
kel, mit E
loath_ed to drink, to drink, they loathed to drink of the ri - ver, they loath
E - kel der Trank, der Trank, mit E - kel er - füll - te der Trank nun, mit E
drink of the ri - ver, they loathed to drink of the ri - ver, they loath - ed, they loath - ed to
füll - te der Trank nun, mit E - kel er - füll - te der Trank nun, mit E - kel, mit E - kel er -
drink, they loathed to drink, they loathed to drink of the ri - ver, they loath - ed, they loath - ed to
Trank, mit E - kel der Trank, mit E - kel er - füll - te der Trank nun, mit E - kel, mit E - kel er -
ed to drink of the ri - ver: He turn_ed their wa - ters in - to blood; they
kel er - füll - te der Trank nun: des Stromes Ge - wäs - ser ward zu Blut; mit
ed to drink of the ri - ver, they loath - ed to drink of the ri - ver, they
kel er - füll - te der Trank nun, mit E - kel er - füll - te der Trank nun, mit
drink of the ri - ver, they loath - ed, they loath
füll - te der Trank nun, mit E - kel, mit E
drink of the ri - ver, of the ri - ver, they loath_ed to
füll - te der Trank, er - füllt' der Trank nun, mit E - kel er

loath - - - - - - - ed to drink of the ri - ver, they loathed, they loath - ed to drink of the
E - - - - - - - kel er - füll - te der Trank nun, mit E - kel, mit E - kel er - füll - te der
loath - ed, they loath - - - ed to drink of the ri - ver, they loath - ed, they
E - kel, mit E - - - kel er - füll - te der Trank nun, mit E - kel, mit
- ed to drink of the ri - ver,
- kel er - füll - te der Trank nun,
drink of the ri - - ver: He turned their wa - ters in - to blood; they
füll - te der Trank nun: des Stromes Ge - wäs - ser ward zu Blut; mit
ri - ver, they loathed, they loath - ed, they loath - ed to drink of the ri - - ver.
Trank nun, mit E - kel, mit E - kel, mit E - kel er - füll - te der Trank nun.
loath - ed to drink of the ri - ver, they loath - ed to drink of the ri - - ver.
E - kel er - füll - te der Trank nun, mit E - kel er - füll - te der Trank nun.
they loath - ed to drink of the ri - - ver.
mit E - kel er - füll - te der Trank nun.
loath - - - - - - - ed, they loath - ed to drink of the ri - - ver.
E - - - - - - - kel, mit E - kel er - füll - te der Trank nun.

Andante.
Violino I.
Violino II.
ALTO.
Bassi.
Andantino.
Pianoforte.
Their
Der
land brought forth frogs, their land brought forth frogs, yea,
Strom zeug - te Frö - sche, die füll - ten das Land, ja,
e - ven in their Kings' cham - bers, yea,
dran - gen in des Kö - nigs Kam - mern, ja,

e - ven in their Kings' cham - - - bers;
dran - gen in des Kö - nigs Kam - - - mern;
their land brought forth frogs, frogs, their land brought forth frogs,
der Strom zeug - te Frösche, Frösche, die füll - ten das Land,
yea, e - ven in their Kings' cham - - - bers, in their
ja, selbst des Kö - nigs Kam - - - mern, des Kö -

Kings' cham - bers.
nigs Kam - mern.
He gave their cat - tle
Er liess von Seu - chen
o - ver to the pes - ti - lence;
schla - gen al - le Heerdentrift;
blot - ches and blains broke forth on man and beast,
schwarzes Ge - schwür brach aus an Mensch und Thier,
mf
mp
6♮
blot - ches and blains,
schwarzes Ge - schwür,
blot - ches and blains broke forth on man and beast, broke
schwarzes Ge - schwür brach aus an Mensch und Thier, brach
p
forth, broke forth on man and beast,
aus, brach aus an Mensch und Thier;

blot - ches and blains, blot - ches and blains broke forth
schwarzes Ge - schwür, schwarzes Ge - schwür brach aus
on man and beast, broke forth
an Mensch und Thier, brach aus
Adagio.
on man and beast.
an Mensch und Thier.
Adagio.
a tempo.
f
mf

CHORUS.

Andante Larghetto.
Trombone I.
Trombone II.
Trombone III.
Oboe I.
Oboe II.
Fagotti.
Violino I.
mezzo piano
Violino II.
Viola.
SOPRANO I.
And there came all man_ner of flies, all manner of
ALTO I.
Und es kam der Fliegen Ge_wühl, der Fliegen Ge_
TENORE I.
He spake the word:
BASSO I.
Er sprach das Wort:
SOPRANO II.
And there came all man_ner of flies, all manner of
ALTO II.
Und es kam der Fliegen Ge_wühl, der Fliegen Ge_
TENORE II.
He spake the word:
BASSO II.
Er sprach das Wort:
Tutti Bassi.
Organo.
Tasto solo.
Soli.
Andante Larghetto.
Pianoforte.

flies,
and there came lice in all their quar_ters;
wühl,
und Mückenschwarm in ih _ re Hö _ fe;
He spake the word:
Er sprach das Wort:
flies,
and there came lice in all their quar_ters;
wühl,
und Mückenschwarm in ih _ re Hö _ fe;
He spake the word:
Er sprach das Wort:
Tasto solo.

forte
and there came all man_ner of flies,
und es kam der Flie_gen Ge_wühl,
He spake the word:
and there came all man_ner of flies,
Er sprach das Wort:
und es kam der Flie_gen Ge_wühl,
He spake the word:
Er sprach das Wort:
Org. I.
f
mf

He spake the word:
He spake the word:
Er sprach das Wort:
Er sprach das Wort:
He spake the word:
He spake the word:
Er sprach das Wort:
Er sprach das Wort:
and there came all man_ner of flies, and there came lice, and there
und es kam der Flie_gen Ge_wühl, der Mü_cken Schwarm, und es
and there came all man_ner of flies, and there came lice, and there
und es kam der Flie_gen Ge_wühl, der Mü_cken Schwarm, und es
Org.II.
Org.II.
Org.II.
Org.I.
Org.I.
cresc.
f
f

and there
und es
and there
und es
came all man_ner of flies, and lice in all their quar - - - ters;
kam der Fliegen und Mü - cken Schwarm in ih - re Hö - - - fe;
came all man_ner of flies, and lice in all their quar - - - ters;
kam der Fliegen und Mü - cken Schwarm in ih - re Hö - - - - fe;
Org. I.

came all manner of flies, and lice in all their quar - - ters; He spake the word:
kam der Fliegen und Mü - cken Schwarm in ih - re Hö - - fe; Er sprach das Wort:
came all manner of flies, and lice in all their quar - - ters; He spake the word:
kam der Fliegen und Mü - cken Schwarm in ih - re Hö - - fe; Er sprach das Wort:
He spake the word: and there
Er sprach das Wort: und es
He spake the word: and there
Er sprach das Wort: und es
Org. II.
Org. I.
Org. II.

and there came all man_ner of flies, and lice in
und es kam der Fliegen und Mü_cken Schwarm in
and there came all man_ner of flies, and lice in
und es kam der Fliegen und Mü_cken Schwarm in
came all man_ner of flies,
kam der Flie_gen Ge_wühl,
came all man_ner of flies,
kam der Flie_gen Ge_wühl,
Org. I.

all their quar - - ters.
He spake the word: and there
ih - re Hö - - fe.
Er sprach das Wort: und es
all their quar - - ters.
He spake the word: and there
ih - re Hö - - fe.
Er sprach das Wort: und es
and lice in all their quar - - ters. He spake the word,
er kam in ih - re Hö - - fe. Er sprach das Wort,
and lice in all their quar - - ters. He spake the word,
er kam in ih - re Hö - - fe. Er sprach das Wort,
Org. II.
Org. I.
Org. II.
Org. I.
f
f

came all manner of flies; He spake the word: and there came all manner of
kam der Fliegen Ge - wühl; Er sprach das Wort: und es kam der Fliegen und
came all manner of flies; He spake the word: and there came all manner of
kam der Fliegen Ge - wühl; Er sprach das Wort: und es kam der Fliegen und
He spake the word, He spake the word:
Er sprach das Wort, Er sprach das Wort:
He spake the word, He spake the word:
Er sprach das Wort, Er sprach das Wort:
Org.II.
Org.I.
f

flies, and lice in all their quar - - - ters.
Mü - cken Schwarm in ih - re Hö - - - fe.
flies, and lice in all their quar - - - ters.
Mü - cken Schwarm in ih - re Hö - - - fe.
and there came all man_ner of
und es kam der Flie_gen und
and there came all man_ner of
und es kam der Flie_gen und
Org. II.

He spake: and the lo - custs came with_out
Er sprach: und der Zug der Heu_schre_cken
He spake: and the lo - custs came with_out
Er sprach: und der Zug der Heu_schre_cken
flies, and lice in all their quar - - - ters. He spake:
Mü - cken Schwarm in ih - re Hö - - - fe. Er sprach:
flies, and lice in all their quar - - - ters. He spake:
Mü - cken Schwarm in ih - re Hö - - - fe. Er sprach:
Org.II.
Org.I.
Tutti.
f
ff

num - ber and de - vour'd the fruits of the ground,
kam und tilg - te al - le Frucht auf dem Feld,
num - ber and de - vour'd the fruits of the ground,
kam und tilg - te al - le Frucht auf dem Feld,
and the lo - custs came with_out
und der Zug der Heu - schrecken
and the lo - custs came with_out
und der Zug der Heu - schrecken
6

and de - vour'd the fruits of the ground.
tilg - - te al - le Frucht auf dem Feld.
and de - vour'd the fruits of the ground.
tilg - - te al - - le Frucht auf dem Feld.
num - ber and de - vour'd the fruits of the ground, and de - vour'd the fruits of the ground.
kam und tilg - te al - le Frucht auf dem Feld, tilg - te al - - le Frucht auf dem Feld.
num - ber and de - vour'd the fruits of the ground, and de - vour'd the fruits of the ground.
kam und tilg - te al - - le Frucht auf dem Feld, tilg - te al - - le Frucht auf dem Feld.
Soli.
mf

Tutti.
Org.
Tutti.

CHORUS.

Allegro.
Oboe I.II.
Fagotti.
Violino I.II.
Viola.
Tutti Bassi, e Organo.
Org. solo.
Tutti.
Allegro.
Pianoforte.
mf
Org. solo.
Tutti.
cresc.

Trombone I.
Trombone II.
Trombone III.
Tromba I.
Tromba II.
Timpani.
Oboe I.
Oboe II.
Fagotti.
Violino I.
Violino II.
Viola.
SOPRANO I.
He gave them hail - stones for rain;
ALTO I.
Er sand - te Ha - gel her - ab;
TENORE I.
He gave them hail - stones for rain;
BASSO I.
Er sand - te Ha - gel her - ab;
SOPRANO II.
He gave them hail - stones for
ALTO II.
Er sand - te Ha - gel - her -
TENORE II.
He gave them hail - stones for
BASSO II.
Er sand - te Ha - gel her -
Tutti Bassi, e Organo.
Org.
ff

fire, mingled with the hail, fire, mingled with the hail, ran a-
rauscht im
Feu'r in dem Ha-gel - sturm, Feu'r in dem Ha-gel - sturm rauscht im
fire, mingled with the hail, fire, mingled with the hail, ran a- -
Feu'r in dem Ha-gel - sturm, Feu'r in dem Ha-gel - sturm ran a-
rauscht im
rain; fire, mingled with the hail, fire, mingled with the hail,
ab; Feu'r in dem Ha-gel - sturm, Feu'r in dem Ha-gel - sturm
rain; fire, mingled with the hail, fire, mingled with the hail,
ab; Feu'r in dem Ha-gel - sturm, Feu'r in dem Ha-gel - sturm
unisoni.

long up - on the ground.
Don - - ner auf das Land.
He gave them hail - stones,
Don-ner auf das Land.
Er sand-te Ha - gel,
long up - on the ground.
He gave them hail - stones,
long up - on the ground.
Don - - ner auf das Land.
Er sand-te Ha - gel,
ran a - long up-on the ground.
He gave them
rauscht im Don - - ner auf das Land.
Er sand-te
ran a - long up-on the ground.
He gave them
rauscht im Don - - ner auf das Land.
Er sand-te

He gave them hail - stones for rain, fire,
Er sand - te Ha - gel her - ab, Feu'r,
He gave them hail - stones for rain, fire,
Er sand - te Ha - gel her - ab, Feu'r,
hail - stones, hail - stones for rain, fire,
Ha - gel, Ha - gel her - ab, Feu'r
hail - stones, hail - stones for rain, fire,
Ha - gel, Ha - gel her - ab, Feu'r,

fire,
ming_led with the hail, ran a - long up_on the ground,
Feu'r
in dem Ha - gelsturm rauscht im Don - ner auf das Land,
fire,
ming_led with the hail, ran a - long up_on the ground,
Feu'r,
fire,
Feu'r
mingled with
in dem Ha -
ming_led with the hail, ran a - long up_on the ground, mingled with
in dem Ha -
in dem Ha - gelsturm rauscht im Don - ner auf das Land,
ming_led with the hail, ran a - long up_on the ground,
fire,
Feu'r
mingled with
in dem Ha -
Organo solo.
Tutti.

ran a - long up - on the ground, mingled with — the hail, ran a -
in dem Ha - - gelsturm rauscht im Don - ner auf das Land, in dem Ha - - gelsturm rauscht im
ming-led with — the hail, ran a - long up - on the ground, mingled with — the hail, ran a -
— the hail,
- gelsturm,
in dem Ha - - gelsturm rauscht im
the hail, ming-led with the hail, ran a - long up - on the ground, mingled with — the hail, ran a -
gel - sturm, in dem Ha-gelsturm
in dem Ha - - gelsturm rauscht im Don - ner auf das Land, in dem Ha - - gelsturm rauscht im
ming-led with — the hail, ran a - long up - on the ground, mingled with — the hail, ran a -
— the hail,
- gelsturm,
in dem Ha - - gelsturm rauscht im
Org. solo.
Tutti.

long up-on the ground. He gave them hail-stones for rain;
Don - ner auf das Land. Er sand-te Ha-gel her-ab;
long up-on the ground. He gave them hail-stones for rain;
Don - ner auf das Land. Er sand-te Ha-gel her-ab;
long up-on the ground. He gave them hail-stones for rain;
Don - ner auf das Land. Er sand-te Ha-gel her-ab;
long up-on the ground. He gave them hail-stones for rain;
Don - ner auf das Land. Er sand-te Ha-gel her-ab;

fire,
ming-led with the hail,
ming-led with the hail,
Feu'r
in dem Ha - gelsturm, with the hail, in dem Sturm, in dem Ha - gel - sturm,
fire,
ming-led with the hail,
ming-led with the hail,
Feu'r
in dem Ha - gel - sturm
ran rauscht
fire, ming-led with the hail,
ming-led with the hail,
Feu'r in dem Ha - gelsturm, with the hail, in dem Sturm, in dem Ha - gel - sturm,
fire, ming-led with the hail,
ming-led with the hail,
Feu'r
in dem Ha - gel - sturm
ran rauscht
Org. solo.
Tutti.

hail, fire, fire, hail - stones ran a - long up - on the
Feu'r, Feu'r, Feu'r, Ha - gel rauscht im Don - ner auf das
hail, fire, fire, hail - stones ran a - long up - on the
im Don - ner auf das
hail, fire, fire, hail - stones ran a - long up - on the
Feu'r, Feu'r, Feu'r, Ha - gel rauscht im Don - ner auf das
hail, fire, fire, hail - stones ran a - long up - on the
im Don - ner auf das

ground, fire, ming-led with the hail, ming-led with the hail,
Land, Feu'r in dem Ha-gel-sturm, in dem Ha-gel-sturm
ground, fire, ming-led with the hail, ming-led with the hail,
Land, Feu'r in dem Ha-gel-sturm, in dem Ha-gel-sturm
ground, fire, ming-led with the hail, ming-led with the hail,
Land, Feu'r in dem Ha-gel-sturm, in dem Ha-gel-sturm
ground, fire, ming-led with the hail, ming-led with the hail,
Land, Feu'r in dem Ha-gel-sturm, in dem Ha-gel-sturm
6

ran a_long up_on the ground, fire, ming_led with the hail, ming_led with
rauscht im Don_ner auf das Land, Feu'r in dem Ha_gel _ sturm, in dem Ha_
ran a_long up_on the ground, fire, ming_led with the hail, ming_led with
rauscht im Don_ner auf das Land, Feu'r in dem Ha_gel _ sturm, in dem Ha_
ran a_long up_on the ground, fire, ming_led with the hail, ming_led with
rauscht im Don_ner auf das Land, Feu'r in dem Ha_gel _ sturm, in dem Ha_
ran a_long up_on the ground, fire, ming_led with the hail, ming_led with
rauscht im Don_ner auf das Land, Feu'r in dem Ha_gel _ sturm, in dem Ha_

the hail, ran a - long up - on the ground, ran a - long up - on the ground.
- gel - sturm rauscht im Don - ner auf das Land, rauscht im Don - ner auf das Land.
the hail, ran a - long up - on the ground, ran a - long up - on the ground.
- gel - sturm rauscht im Don - ner auf das Land, rauscht im Don - ner auf das Land.
the hail, ran a - long up - on the ground, ran a - long up - on the ground.
- gel - sturm rauscht im Don - ner auf das Land, rauscht im Don - ner auf das Land.
the hail, ran a - long up - on the ground, ran a - long up - on the ground.
- gel - sturm rauscht im Don - ner auf das Land, rauscht im Don - ner auf das Land.
mf

(Tutti Bassi, e Organo.)

CHORUS.

Largo.
Violino I.
Violino II.
Viola.
Fagotto I.II.
SOPRANO.
ALTO.
TENORE.
BASSO.
Tutti Bassi.
Largo, non adagio.
Pianoforte.
p
He sent a thick dark - ness o-ver all the land, o-ver all the land,
Er sand-te di-cke Finsterniss ü-ber all das Land, ü-ber all das Land,
He sent a thick dark - ness o-ver all the land, o-ver all the land,
Er sand-te di-cke Finsterniss ü-ber all das Land, ü-ber all das Land,

e-ven dark-ness, which might be felt, a thick dark - - - ness He sent
di-cke Fin - - - sterniss Er sandt'
di-cke Finsterniss, dass nie-mand sah, a thick dark-ness, He sent a thick
di-cke Finsterniss, Er sand - - - te di-cke
e-ven dark-ness, which might be felt; He sent a thick
Er sand - - - te di-cke
di-cke Finsterniss, dass nie-mand sah; He sent
Er sandt'
o-ver all the land,
ü-ber all das Land,
dark-ness
Finsterniss
dark-ness,
Finsterniss,
e'en dark-ness, which might be
ein Dun-kel, dass nie-mand
a thick dark-ness o'er all the land,
di-cke Finsterniss auf all das Land,
cresc.

a thick darkness
tie-fes Nachtgrau'n
o'er all the land,
auf all das Land,
felt,
sah,
even darkness, which might be felt,
di-cke Finsterniss, dass nie-mand sah,
a
ein
a thick dark-ness,
di-cke Finsterniss,
Ped.
o'er all the land
auf all das Land
darkness,
Dun-kel,
which might be felt.
dass nie-mand sah.
e-ven darkness, which might be felt.
di-cke Finsterniss, dass nie-mand sah.
Ped.
decresc.
pp

CHORUS.

A tempo giusto, e staccato.
Trombone I.
Trombone II.
Trombone III.
Oboe I.
Oboe II.
Fagotto I.
Fagotto II.
Violino I.
Violino II.
Viola.
SOPRANO.
He smote all the first-born of E - gypt, the chief of all their strength,
Erschlug al-le Erstgeburt Aegyp - tens, den Kern der gan - zen Macht,
ALTO.
The chief of all their strength, the chief, the
Den Kern der gan - - - - zen Macht, den Kern, den
TENORE.
BASSO.
He smote all the
Er schlug al-le
Tutti Bassi.
A tempo giusto, e staccato.
Pianoforte.

of all their strength,
der ganzen Macht,
the chief of all their strength, of all their
den Kern der gan-zen Macht, der gan - zen
chief of all, of all their strength,
Kern der gan - - - - - - - zen, gan-zen Macht,
the chief of all their
den Kern der gan-zen
The chief of all their strength, the chief of all their strength;
Den Kern der gan - - - - zen Macht, den Kern der gan-zen Macht;
first-born in E - gypt, the chief of all their strength,
Erstgeburt Aegyp - tens, den Kern der gan - zen Macht,
the chief of all their
den Kern der gan-zen

strength, of all their strength, the chief of all their strength, the chief of all their
Macht, der gan - - - - - zen Macht, den Kern der gan - zen Macht, den Kern der gan - zen
strength, the chief, the chief of all, of all their strength,
Macht, den Kern, den Kern der gan - - zen, ganzen Macht,
He smote all the first - born of E - gypt, the chief of all their strength,
Er schlug al - le Erstgeburt Ae - gyp - tens, den Kern der gan - zen Macht,
strength, the chief of all their strength, the chief of all their
Macht, den Kern der gan - - - - zen Macht, den Kern der gan - zen

strength, the chief of all their
Macht, den Kern der gan_zen
strength,
Macht,
the chief of all their
den Kern der gan - - - zen
the chief of all their
den Kern der gan_zen
strength, of all their
Macht, der gan - - - zen
the chief of all their
den Kern der gan_zen
strength, of all their
Macht, der gan_zen
strength,
Macht,
the chief,
den Kern,
strength;
Macht;
He smote all the
Er schlug al_le
first-born of E - gypt,
Erstgeburt Aegyp - tens,
the chief of all their
den Kern der gan_zen

strength,
Macht,
the chief of all, the chief of all their
den Kern der gan - zen Macht, den Kern der gan-zen
strength, the chief of all their strength,
Macht, den Kern der ganzen Macht,
the chief of all their strength,
den Kern der gan - zen Macht,
the chief of all
den Kern der gan -
the chief of all their strength, the chief of all, of all their strength,
den Kern der ganzen Macht, den Kern der gan - zen, gan - zen Macht,
strength,
Macht,
the chief of all their strength;
den Kern der gan-zen Macht;

strength, of all their strength; He smote all the first - born of E -
Macht, der gan - zen Macht; Er schlug al - le Erst - geburt Aegyp -
their strength, the chief of all their
zen Macht, den Kern der gan - zen
the chief of all their strength,
den Kern der gan - zen Macht,
He smote all the first - born of E - gypt,
Er schlug al - le Erstgeburt Aegyp - tens,
7 3 4 2 6 4 2 6

gypt, the chief of all their strength,
tens, den Kern der gan - - - zen Macht,
strength;
Macht;
He smote all the first - born of E -
Er schlug al - le Erstgeburt Ae-gyp -
the chief of all
den Kern der gan -
the chief of all their strength,
den Kern der gan - zen Macht,

the chief of all their
den Kern der gan-zen
strength,
Macht,
the chief of
den Kern der
all
gan - - - - - zen
their
strength;
Macht;
He smote all the
Er schlug al-le
gypt,
tens,
the chief
den Kern
of all
der gan
their
zen
strength;
Macht;
He
Er
their
zen
strength,
Macht,
the chief of all
den Kern der gan
their
zen
strength,
Macht,
the chief of all their
den Kern der gan-zen
strength,
Macht,
the chief of
den Kern der
all
gan - - zen
their
strength;
Macht;

first - born of E - gypt,
Erstgeburt Ae-gyp - tens,
the chief of all their
den Kern der gan - zen
strength, the chief of all their
Macht, den Kern der gan - zen
smote all the first - born of E - gypt,
schlug al - le Erst - ge - burt Ae-gyp - tens,
the chief of all their
den Kern der gan - zen
the chief of all their strength, of all their strength, of all their
den Kern der gan - zen Macht, der gan - zen Macht, der gan - zen
He smote all the first - born of E - gypt, the chief of all their
Er schlug al - le Erstgeburt Ae - gyp - tens, den Kern der gan - zen

strength. He smote the chief of all their strength, He smote the
Macht.
strength. Er schlug den Kern der gan - zen Macht, Er schlug den
Macht.
strength. He smote the chief of all their strength, He smote the
Macht.
strength. Er schlug den Kern der gan - zen Macht, Er schlug den
Macht.

chief of all their strength. He smote all the first - born of E - gypt,
Er schlug al - le Erstgeburt Ae - gyp - tens,
Kern der gan - zen Macht. He smote all the first-born of E - gypt, the chief of their
Er schlug al - le Erstgeburt Ae - gyp - tens, den Kern ih - rer
chief of all their strength. He
Er
Kern der gan - zen Macht. He smote all the
Er schlug al - le

the chief of all their
den Kern der gan-zen
strength,
Macht,
the chief of all
den Kern der gan
strength, of their
gan - - - zen
strength,
Macht,
the chief of all
den Kern der gan
smote all the first - born,
schlug al - le Erstge - burt,
the chief of all
den Kern der gan
(of all their strength, the chief, the
(zen Macht, den Kern der
first-born of E - gypt,
Erstgeburt Aegyp - tens,
the chief of all,
den Kern der gan

their strength. He smote all the first - born of E - gypt, the chief, the chief of all their
- - - - zen Macht.
their strength. Er schlug al-le Erstgeburt Aegyp - tens, den Kern, den Kern der gan-zen
- - - - zen Macht.
chief of all) their strength. He smote all the first - born of E - gypt, the chief, the chief of all their
gan) - - - zen Macht.
of all their strength. Er schlug al-le Erstgeburt Aegyp - tens, den Kern, den Kern der gan - zen
- zen, gan - zen Macht.
ritard.

strength.
Macht.
strength.
Macht.
6
a tempo.
decresc.

CHORUS.
Andante.
Oboe I.II.
Fagotto I.II.
Violino I.
Violino II.
Viola.
SOPRANO.
But as for His people, but as for His people,
ALTO.
Doch mit dem Volk Is_rael, doch mit dem Volk Is_rael He zog
TENORE.
But as for His people, but as for His people,
BASSO.
Doch mit dem Volk Is_rael, doch mit dem Volk Is_rael
Tutti Bassi.
Andante con moto.
Pianoforte.
e Flauto traverso.
e Flauto traverso.
He led, He led them
zog Er da - hin gleich
led, He led them forth like sheep,
Er da - hin gleich wie ein Hirt,

forth like sheep,
wie ein Hirt,
He
zog
He led, He led them forth like sheep,
zog Er da - hin gleich wie ein Hirt,
6 4♮
6 4♮
5 3
6 4♮
He led, He led them
zog Er da - hin gleich
led them forth,
Er da - hin,
He led them forth,
zog Er da - hin,
He led, He led them forth like sheep,
zog Er da - hin gleich wie ein Hirt,

forth like sheep,
wie ein Hirt,
like sheep.
ein Hirt.
He led them forth like sheep.
zog Er gleich wie ein Hirt.
He led, He led them forth like sheep.
zog Er da - hin gleich wie ein Hirt.
like sheep.
ein Hirt.
But as for His people, but as for His people, He brought them out with
Er führt' es hin - aus mit
Er führ-te Sein Is-rael, Er führte Sein Is-rael,
But as for His people, but as for His people,
Er führ-te Sein Is-rael, Er führte Sein Is-rael,
forte
Tasto solo.
f
mf

sil-ver and gold, He brought them out with sil-ver and gold,
Sil-ber und Gold, Er führt' es aus mit Sil-ber und Gold,
He brought them out with sil-ver and gold, with sil-ver and gold,
Er führt'es hin-aus mit Sil-ber und Gold, mit Sil-ber und Gold.
He
Er
unis.
with sil-ver and gold, with sil-ver and gold, He brought them
mit Sil-ber und Gold, mit Sil-ber und Gold, Er führt' es
He brought, He brought them out with sil-ver and gold,
Er führt', Er führt'es hin-aus mit Sil-ber und Gold,
brought them out with sil-ver and gold, He brought them
führt' es hin-aus mit Sil-ber und Gold, Er führt' es
He brought them out with sil-ver and gold,
Er führt'es hin-aus mit Sil-ber und Gold,
7 6

out,
aus,
He brought them
Er führt' es
out with
aus mit
sil - ver and
Sil - ber und
gold, He
Gold, Er
brought,
führt;
He
Er
brought
führt'
He brought them
Er führt' es
out with
aus mit
sil - ver and
Sil - ber und
gold, He
Gold, Er
brought
führt'
out, He
aus, Er
brought them
führt' es
out with
aus mit
sil - ver and
Sil - ber und
gold, He
Gold, Er
brought
führt'
them
es
He brought them
Er führt' es
out
aus
with
mit
sil - ver and
Sil - ber und
gold,
Gold,
them
es
out,
aus,
He
Er
brought them
führt'es hin -
out with
aus mit
sil - ver and
Sil - ber und
them
es
out with
aus mit
sil - ver and
Sil - ber und
gold, He
Gold, Er
brought
führt'
them
es
out with
aus mit
sil - ver and
Sil - ber und
out
aus
with
mit
sil - ver and
Sil - ber und
gold, with
Gold, mit
sil - ver and
Sil - ber und
gold,
Gold,
He
Er
brought them
führt'es hin -
out with
aus mit
sil - ver and
Sil - ber und
gold,
Gold,
He
Er
brought them
führt'es hin -

gold, He brought them out. He brought
Gold, Er führt' es hin aus, Er führt'
gold, and gold,
Gold, und Gold,
He brought
Er führt'
out with sil - ver and gold, He brought
aus mit Sil - ber und Gold, Er führt'
them out, He brought them out with sil - ver and gold,
es aus, Er führt' es hin - aus mit Sil - ber und Gold,
He brought them out with sil - ver and gold, with sil - ver and
Er führt' es hin - aus mit Sil - ber und Gold, mit Sil - ber und
them out, He brought them out with sil - ver and gold,
es aus, Er führt' es hin - aus mit Sil - ber und Gold,
them out, He brought them
es aus, Er führt' es hin -

He brought them out with
Er führt'es hin - aus mit
gold, He brought them out with sil-ver and gold, He brought them out
Gold, Er führt' es aus mit Sil-ber und Gold, Er führt' es aus
He brought them out with sil-ver and gold,
Er führt' es aus mit Sil-ber und Gold,
out with sil-ver and gold, He brought them out with sil-ver and
aus mit Sil-ber und Gold, Er führt' es aus mit Sil-ber und
sil-ver and gold. But as for His people, but as for His people,
Sil-ber und Gold.
with sil-ver and gold. Doch mit dem Volk Is-rael, doch mit dem Volk Is-rael
mit Sil-ber und Gold.
with sil-ver and gold. But as for His people, but as for His people,
mit Sil-ber und Gold.
gold, with sil - ver and gold. Doch mit dem Volk Is-rael, doch mit dem Volk Is-rael He
Gold, mit Sil - ber und Gold. zog
f
p

He led them forth like sheep, like sheep;
zog Er gleich wie ein Hirt, ein Hirt;
He led, He led them forth like sheep;
zog Er da-hin gleich wie ein Hirt;
He led them forth like sheep, like sheep;
zog Er gleich wie ein Hirt, ein Hirt;
led, He led them forth like sheep;
Er da-hin gleich wie ein Hirt;
He brought them out with sil-ver and gold, He
Er führt'es hin-aus mit Sil-ber und Gold, Er
He brought them out with sil-ver and gold,
Er führt'es hin-aus mit Sil-ber und Gold,
He
Er
mf

brought them out, He brought them out, He brought them out
führt' es hin - aus, Er führt' es aus, Er führt' es aus
He brought them out, He brought, He brought them
Er führt' es aus, Er führt', Er führt' es
brought them out with sil - ver and gold, He brought, He brought them
führt' es hin - aus mit Sil - ber und Gold, Er führt', Er führt' es
He brought them out with sil - ver and gold,
Er führt' es hin - aus mit Sil - ber und Gold,
with sil - ver and gold: there was not one, not one fee - ble per - son a - mong their
out mit Sil - ber und Gold: führ - te das gan - ze Heer aus Ae - gyp - ten auf Ei - nen
out with sil - ver and gold: there was not one, not one fee - ble per - son a - mong their
mit Sil - ber und Gold: führ - te das gan - ze Heer aus Ae - gyp - ten auf Ei - nen

tribes, there was not one, not one fee_ble per_son a_mong their tribes, not one fee_ble
Tag, führ_te das gan_ze Heer aus Ae_gyp_ten auf Ei_nen Tag, das gan_ze
tribes, there was not one, not one fee_ble per_son a_mong their tribes, not one fee_ble
Tag, führ_te das gan_ze Heer aus Ae_gyp_ten auf Ei_nen Tag, das gan_ze
per_son, there was not one, not one fee_ble per_son a_mong their tribes.
Heer führt Er aus, das gan_ze Heer aus Ae_gyp_ten auf Ei_nen Tag.
per_son, there was not one, not one fee_ble per_son a_mong their tribes.
Heer führt Er aus, das gan_ze Heer aus Ae_gyp_ten auf Ei_nen Tag.
mf

CHORUS.
A tempo giusto.
Oboe I.
Oboe II.
Fagotto I.
Fagotto II.
SOPRANO.
ALTO.
TENORE.
BASSO.
Tutti Bassi.
Organo tasto solo senza altri Bassi.
Pianoforte.
E - gypt was glad when they de - par - ted,
Froh sah Ae - gyp - ten sei - nen Aus - zug,

E - gypt was glad when they de - par - ted, E - gypt was glad when they de -
Froh sah Ae - gyp - ten sei - nen Aus - zug, froh sah Ae - gyp - ten sei - nen
ted, E - gypt was glad when they de - par - ted,
zug, froh sah Ae - gyp - ten sei - nen Aus - zug,
par - ted, E - gypt was glad when they de - par
Aus - zug, froh sah Ae - gyp - ten sei - nen Aus
E - gypt was glad when they de - par
froh sah Ae - gyp - ten sei - nen Aus
Tutti Bassi.
par - ted, when they de - par - ted, E - gypt was
Aus - zug, froh sei - nen Aus - zug, froh sah Ae -
E - gypt was glad when they de - par
froh sah Ae - gyp - ten sei - nen Aus
ted, when they de - par
zug, froh sei - nen Aus
ted, E -
zug, froh
(Org. tasto solo.)
(Tutti Bassi.)

Trombone I.
Trombone II.
Trombone III.
Oboe I.
Oboe II.
Fagotto I.
Fagotto II.
Violino I.
Violino II.
Viola.
SOPRANO.
glad when they de - par - ted,
gyp-ten sei-nen Aus - zug,
ALTO.
ted,
zug,
TENORE.
ted, for the fear of them fell up - on them,
zug, denn die Furcht vor ihm ü - ber - kam sie,
BASSO.
gypt was glad when they de-par - ted, for the fear of them
sah Ae - gyp-ten sei-nen Aus - zug, denn die Furcht vor ihm
Org. tasto solo.
Tutti Bassi.

for the fear of them
denn die Furcht vor ihm
fell up - on
ü - ber - kam
E - gypt was
froh sah Ae -
glad when they de -
gyp - ten sei - nen
par - - - - - - - - - - - - - -
Aus - - - - - - - - - - - - - -
fell up - on
ü - ber - kam
them,
sie,
for the fear fell up - on them,
denn die Furcht ü - ber - kam sie,
fell up - on
ü - ber - kam
them,
sie,
E - gypt was
froh sah Ae -
Tutti Bassi.
Senza Bassi.

them,
sie,
E - gypt was glad when they de - par - - - - - -
froh sah Ae - gyp-ten sei - nen Aus - - - - -
- - - - - - - - - - - - - - - - - - - ted,
- - - - - - - - - - - - - - - - - - - zug,
for the fear fell up - on them, the fear fell up -
denn die Furcht ü - ber - kam sie, die Furcht ü - ber -
for the fear of them fell up - on
denn die Furcht vor ihm ü - berkam
them,
sie,
glad when they de - par - - - - - - - - - - ted,
gyp-ten sei - nen Aus - - - - - - - - - - zug,
(Org. tasto solo.)

ted,
zug,
on them, the fear fell up - on them,
kam sie, die Furcht ü - ber - kam sie,
for the fear fell up - on them, the fear fell up -
denn die Furcht ü - ber - kam sie, die Furcht ü - ber -
E - gypt was glad when they de - par
froh sah Ae - gyp - ten sei - nen Aus

E - gypt was glad when they de - par - - - - - - - - - -
froh sah Ae - gyp - ten sei - nen Aus - - - - - - - - - -
E - - gypt was glad when they de - par - - ted, for the fear of them fell up - on them;
froh sah Ae - gyp - ten sei - nen Aus - - zug, denn die Furcht vor ihm ü - berkam sie;
on them, the fear of them fell up - on them, for the fear of them fell up - on
kam sie, die Furcht vor ihm ü - ber - kam sie, denn die Furcht vor ihm ü - - - ber - kam

ted,
zug,
E - gypt was glad when they de - par - - -
froh sah Ae - gyp - ten sei - nen Aus - - -
E - gypt was glad when they de - par - ted, for the fear of them fell up - on
froh sah Ae - gyp - ten sei - nen Aus - zug, denn die Furcht vor ihm ü - ber - kam
them, for the fear of them fell up - on them,
sie, denn die Furcht vor ihm ü - ber - kam sie,
- - - - ted, for the fear of them fell up - on
- - - - zug, denn die Furcht vor ihm ü - ber - kam

ted, for the fear of them fell up - on them, fell up - on
zug, denn die Furcht vor ihm ü - ber - kam sie, ü - ber-kam
them, for the fear fell up - on them,
sie, denn die Furcht ü - ber - kam sie,
for the fear of them fell up - on them, for the fear, for the fear of them
denn die Furcht vor ihm ü - ber - kam sie, denn die Furcht, denn die Furcht vor ihm
them, for the fear
sie, denn die Furcht

them, for the
sie, denn die
fear of them fell up -
Furcht vor ihm ü - ber -
for the fear of them
denn die Furcht vor ihm
fell up - on
ü - ber - kam
them, fell up - on
sie, ü - ber - kam
them,
sie,
fell up - on
ü - ber - kam
them, for the fear of them
sie, denn die Furcht vor ihm
fell up - on them,
ü - ber - kam sie,
for the fear fell up -
denn die Furcht ü - ber -
of them
vor ihm
fell
ü
up - -
ber - -
on
kam

on them, for the
kam sie, denn die
fear of them fell up - on
Furcht vor ihm ü - ber - kam
them.
sie.
for the fear fell up - on them,
denn die Furcht ü - ber - kam sie,
fell up - on
ü - ber - kam
them.
sie.
on them,
kam sie,
for the fear fell up - on
denn die Furcht ü - ber - kam
them.
sie.
them.
sie.

CHORUS.

Grave, e staccato.

Oboe I.
Oboe II.
Fagotto I.
Fagotto II.
Violino I.
Violino II.
Viola.

SOPRANO I.
He re - bu - ked the Red Sea, and it was dri - ed up.

ALTO I.
Er ge - bot es der Meer - flut: und sie trock - ne - te aus.

TENORE I.
He re - bu - ked the Red Sea, and it was dri - ed up.

BASSO I.
Er ge - bot es der Meer - flut: und sie trock - ne - te aus.

SOPRANO II.
He re - bu - ked the Red Sea, and it was dri - ed up.

ALTO II.
Er ge - bot es der Meer - flut: und sie trock - ne - te aus.

TENORE II.
He re - bu - ked the Red Sea, and it was dri - ed up.

BASSO II.
Er ge - bot es der Meer - flut: und sie trock - ne - te aus.

Tutti Bassi.
Organo.

Grave, e staccato.

Pianoforte.

ff

p

He re - bu - ked the Red Sea, and it was dri - ed up.
Er ge - bot es der Meer - flut: und sie trock - ne - te aus.
ff
p

A tempo giusto.
Oboe I.
Oboe II.
Fagotti.
Violino I.
Violino II.
Viola.
SOPRANO I.
ALTO I.
TENORE I.
BASSO I.
He led them through the deep, He led them through the deep as
Er führ - te durch die Tie - fe tro - cken sie hin - durch wie
SOPRANO II.
ALTO II.
TENORE II.
BASSO II.
He led them through the deep, He led them through the deep as
Er führ - te durch die Tie - fe tro - cken sie hin - durch wie
Tutti Bassi.
Organo.
Tasto solo.
A tempo giusto.
Pianoforte.

He led them through the deep, He led them through the deep as
Er führ-te durch die Tie-fe tro-cken sie hin-durch wie
through a wil-der-ness,
durch ein Wü-sten-land,
He led them through the deep, He led them through the deep as
Er führ-te durch die Tie-fe tro-cken sie hin-durch wie
through a wil-der-ness,
durch ein Wü-sten-land,

He
led them through the
deep, He led them
Er
führ - te durch die
Tie - - fe tro - - cken
through a wil - derness,
as thro' a
wil - derness,
as thro' a
durch ein Wü - stenland,
wie durch ein
Wü - stenland,
wie durch ein
as thro' a wil - der - ness,
as thro' a wil - der - ness,
wie durch ein Wü - stenland,
wie durch ein Wü - sten - land,
He
led them through the
deep, He led them
Er
führ - te durch die
Tie - - fe tro - - cken
through a wil - derness,
as thro' a
wil - der - ness,
as thro' a
durch ein Wü - stenland,
wie durch ein
Wü - sten - land,
wie durch ein
as thro' a wil - der - ness,
as thro' a wil - der - ness,
wie durch ein Wü - stenland,
wie durch ein Wü - sten - land,

He led them through the
Er führ - te durch die
through the deep as thro' a wil - der - ness, as thro' a
sie hin - durch wie durch ein Wü - stenland, wie durch ein
wil - derness, as through a wil - der - ness,
Wü - stenland, wie durch ein Wü - sten - land,
as thro' a wil - der - ness, as through a wil - der - ness, as thro' a wil - derness, He
wie durch ein Wü - stenland, wie durch ein Wü - sten - land, wie durch ein Wü - stenland, Er
He led them as thro' a
Er führt' sie wie durch ein
through the deep as thro' a wil - der - ness,
sie hin durch wie durch ein Wü - stenland,
wil - derness, as through a wil - derness, as thro' a wil - derness,
Wü - stenland, wie durch ein Wü - stenland, wie durch ein Wü - stenland,
as thro' a wil - der - ness, as through a wil - der - ness, as thro' a wil - derness, He
wie durch ein Wü - stenland, wie durch ein Wü - sten - land, wie durch ein Wü - stenland, Er

deep, He led them through the deep as thro' a wil - derness,
Tie - - fe tro - - cken sie hin - durch wie durch ein Wü - stenland,
wil - derness, as thro' a wil - derness, He led them as thro' a wil - derness,
Wü - stenland, wie durch ein Wü - stenland, Er führt' sie wie durch ein Wü - stenland,
as thro' a wil - der - ness, as thro' a wil - der - ness, as thro' a wil - der - ness,
wie durch ein Wü - stenland, wie durch ein Wü - stenland, wie durch ein Wü - stenland,
led them through the deep, thro' the deep as thro' a wil - - derness, as thro' a
führ - - te durch die Tie - - fe hin - durch wie durch ein Wü - - stenland, wie durch ein
wil - derness, He led them through the deep as thro' a wil - der - ness, as thro' a
Wü - stenland, Er führ - - te sie hin - durch wie durch ein Wü - stenland, wie durch ein
as thro' a wil - der - ness, He led them as thro' a wil - derness,
wie durch ein Wü - stenland, Er führt' sie wie durch ein Wü - stenland,
as thro' a wil - derness, He led them as thro' a wil - derness,
wie durch ein Wü - stenland, Er führt' sie wie durch ein Wü - stenland,
led them through the deep, thro' the deep as thro' a wil - - derness, as thro' a
führ - - te durch die Tie - - fe hin - durch wie durch ein Wü - - stenland, wie durch ein

as thro' a wil_der_ness, He led them through the
wie durch ein Wü_stenland, Er führ_te durch die
as thro' a wil_derness, He led them through the
wie durch ein Wü_stenland, Er führ_te sie hin_
as thro' a wil_ _derness, as thro' a wil_ _ _derness,
wie durch ein Wü_ _stenland, wie durch ein Wü_ _ _stenland,
wil_der_ness, He led them thro' the
Wü_stenland, Er führ_ _ _te durch die
wil_derness, as thro' a wil_der_ness, as thro' a
Wü_stenland, wie durch ein Wü_stenland, wie durch ein
as thro' a wil_derness, He led them thro' the
wie durch ein Wü_stenland, Er führ_te sie hin_
as thro' a wil_derness, as thro' a wil_ _ _derness,
wie durch ein Wü_stenland, wie durch ein Wü_ _ _stenland,
wil_derness, He led them thro' the
Wü_stenland, Er führ_ _ _te durch die

deep, He led them through the deep as thro' a wil_derness,
Tie_ _fe tro_ _cken sie hin_ _durch wie durch ein Wü_stenland,
deep as thro' a wil_der_ness, as thro' a wil_ _der_ness,
durch wie durch ein Wü_stenland, wie durch ein Wü_ _sten_land,
as thro' a wil_der_ness, as thro' a wil_derness, as thro' a wilder_ness, as thro' a
wie durch ein Wü_stenland, wie durch ein Wü_stenland, wie durch ein Wüsten_land, wie durch ein
deep, He led them through the deep as thro' a wil_der_ness, as thro' a
Tie_ _fe tro_ _cken sie hin_ _durch wie durch ein Wü_stenland, wie durch ein
wil_der_ness, as thro' a wil_der_ness, as thro' a wil_der_ness,
Wü_stenland, wie durch ein Wü_stenland, wie durch ein Wü_stenland,
Tasto solo.

as thro' a wil_derness, as thro' a wil_derness,
wie durch ein Wü_stenland, wie durch ein Wü_stenland,
as thro' a wil_derness, He led them through the deep
wie durch ein Wü_stenland, Er führ_ _te sie hin_ _durch
wil_derness, as thro' a wil_derness, as thro' a
Wü_stenland, wie durch ein Wü_stenland, wie durch ein
wil_derness, He led them through the deep as thro' a wil_derness,
Wü_stenland, Er führ_ _te sie hin_ _durch wie durch ein Wü_stenland,
as thro' a wil_derness, as thro' a wil_der_ness,
wie durch ein Wü_stenland, wie durch ein Wü_stenland,
as thro' a wil_der_ness, He led them through the deep as
wie durch ein Wü_stenland, Er führ_ _te sie hin_ _durch wie
wil_der_ness, as thro' a wil_der_ness, as thro' a
Wü_stenland, wie durch ein Wü_stenland, wie durch ein
wil_der_ness, He led them through the deep as thro' a wil_derness,
Wü_stenland, Er führ_ _te sie hin_ _durch wie durch ein Wü_stenland,

as thro' a wil-der- ness, a wil-der-ness, as thro' a wil-derness, as
wie durch ein Wü - sten- land, ein Wü-stenland, wie durch ein Wüstenland, wie
as thro' a wil-derness, as thro' a wil-derness, as thro' a wilderness,
wie durch ein Wü-stenland, wie durch ein Wü-stenland, wie durch ein Wüstenland,
wil-derness, as thro' a wil-derness, thro' a wil-derness,
Wüstenland, wie durch ein Wüstenland, durch ein Wü-stenland,
as through a wil- - -derness, He led them through the
wie durch ein Wü- - -stenland, Er führ- -te durch die
as thro' a wil-derness, as thro' a wilderness, as thro' a
wie durch ein Wüstenland, wie durch ein Wüstenland, wie durch ein
thro' a wilderness, as thro' a wil-derness, as thro' a wilderness,
durch ein Wüstenland, wie durch ein Wü-stenland, wie durch ein Wüstenland,
wil-derness, as thro' a wilderness, thro' a wil-derness,
Wüstenland, wie durch ein Wüstenland, durch ein Wüstenland,
as through a wil- - -derness, He led them through the
wie durch ein Wü- - -stenland, Er führ- -te durch die
cresc.

thro' a wil-der-ness, He led them through the deep as thro' a wil-der-ness.
durch ein Wü-sten-land, Er führ-te sie hindurch wie durch ein Wü-sten-land.
as thro' a wil-der-ness, He led them through the deep as thro' a wil-der-ness.
wie durch ein Wü-sten-land, Er führ-te sie hindurch wie durch ein Wü-sten-land.
as thro' a wil-der-ness, He led them through the deep as thro' a wil-der-ness.
wie durch ein Wü-sten-land, Er führ-te sie hindurch wie durch ein Wü-sten-land.
deep, He led them through the deep as thro' a wil-der-ness.
Tie-fe tro-cken sie hin-durch wie durch ein Wü-sten-land.
wil-der-ness, He led them through the deep as thro' a wil-der-ness.
Wü-sten-land, Er führ-te sie hin-durch wie durch ein Wü-sten-land.
He led them through the deep as thro' a wil-der-ness.
Er führ-te sie hin-durch wie durch ein Wü-sten-land.
as thro' a wil-der-ness, He led them through the deep as thro' a wil-der-ness.
wie durch ein Wü-sten-land, Er führ-te sie hin-durch wie durch ein Wü-sten-land.
deep, He led them through the deep as thro' a wil-der-ness.
Tie-fe tro-cken sie hin-durch wie durch ein Wü-sten-land.

(a Tempo giusto.)
Timpani.
Oboe I.II.
Violino I.II.
Viola.
SOPRANO.
ALTO.
TENORE.
BASSO.
Tutti Bassi.
Pianoforte.
But the waters o - verwhelmed their e - nemies, o - ver-
Doch die Feinde ü - ber-ström-te die Was - ser-flut, ü - ber-
whelm - - ed their e - nemies, there was not one of them left, there was not one, not
ström - - te die Was-serflut, dass auch nicht Ei - ner entkam, dass auch nicht Ei - ner,

one, there was not one of them left, there was not one of them left, not one, not
auch nicht, auch nicht Ei - ner ent - kam, dass auch nicht Ei - ner ent - kam, nicht Ei - ner ent -
one, there was not one of them left, there was not one of them left, not one, not
auch nicht, auch nicht Ei - ner ent - kam, dass auch nicht Ei - ner ent - kam, nicht Ei - ner ent -
one, there was not one, not one, not one, there was not one, there was not
kam, dass auch nicht Ei - ner, nicht Ei - ner ent - kam, dass auch nicht Ei - ner, dass auch nicht
one, there was not one, not one, not one, there was not one, there was not
kam, dass auch nicht Ei - ner, nicht Ei - ner ent - kam, dass auch nicht Ei - ner, dass auch nicht

one, not one of them left, there was not one, not one of them left, there was not
Ei_ner, nicht Ei_ner ent_kam, dass auch nicht, auch nicht Ei_ner ent_kam, dass auch nicht
one, not one of them left, there was not one, not one of them left, there was not
Ei_ner, nicht Ei_ner ent_kam, dass auch nicht, auch nicht Ei_ner ent_kam, dass auch nicht
one, not one of them left: the wa_ters o - verwhelmed their e_nemies, o_ver - whelm - ed their
Einer, nicht Ei_ner ent_kam: die Fein_de ü - berströmte die Was_serflut, ü - ber_ström - te die
one, not one of them left: the wa_ters o - verwhelmed their e_nemies, o_ver - whelm - ed their
Einer, nicht Ei_ner ent_kam: die Fein_de ü - berströmte die Was_serflut, ü - ber_ström - te die

e - nemies, there was not one left, there was not one, there was not one, not
Was - serflut, nicht Ei - ner ent - kam, nicht Ei - ner ent - kam, dass auch nicht Ei - ner ent -
e - nemies, there was not one left, there was not one, there was not one, not
Was - serflut, nicht Ei - ner ent - kam, nicht Ei - ner ent - kam, dass auch nicht Ei - ner ent -
con 8va ad libit.
one, there was not one, not one of them left, not one, there was not one of them left.
kam, dass auch nicht Ei - ner, nicht Ei - ner ent - kam, nicht Ei - ner, dass auch nicht Ei - ner ent - kam.
one, there was not one, not one of them left, not one, there was not one of them left.
kam, dass auch nicht Ei - ner, nicht Ei - ner ent - kam, nicht Ei - ner, dass auch nicht Ei - ner ent - kam.

CHORUS.

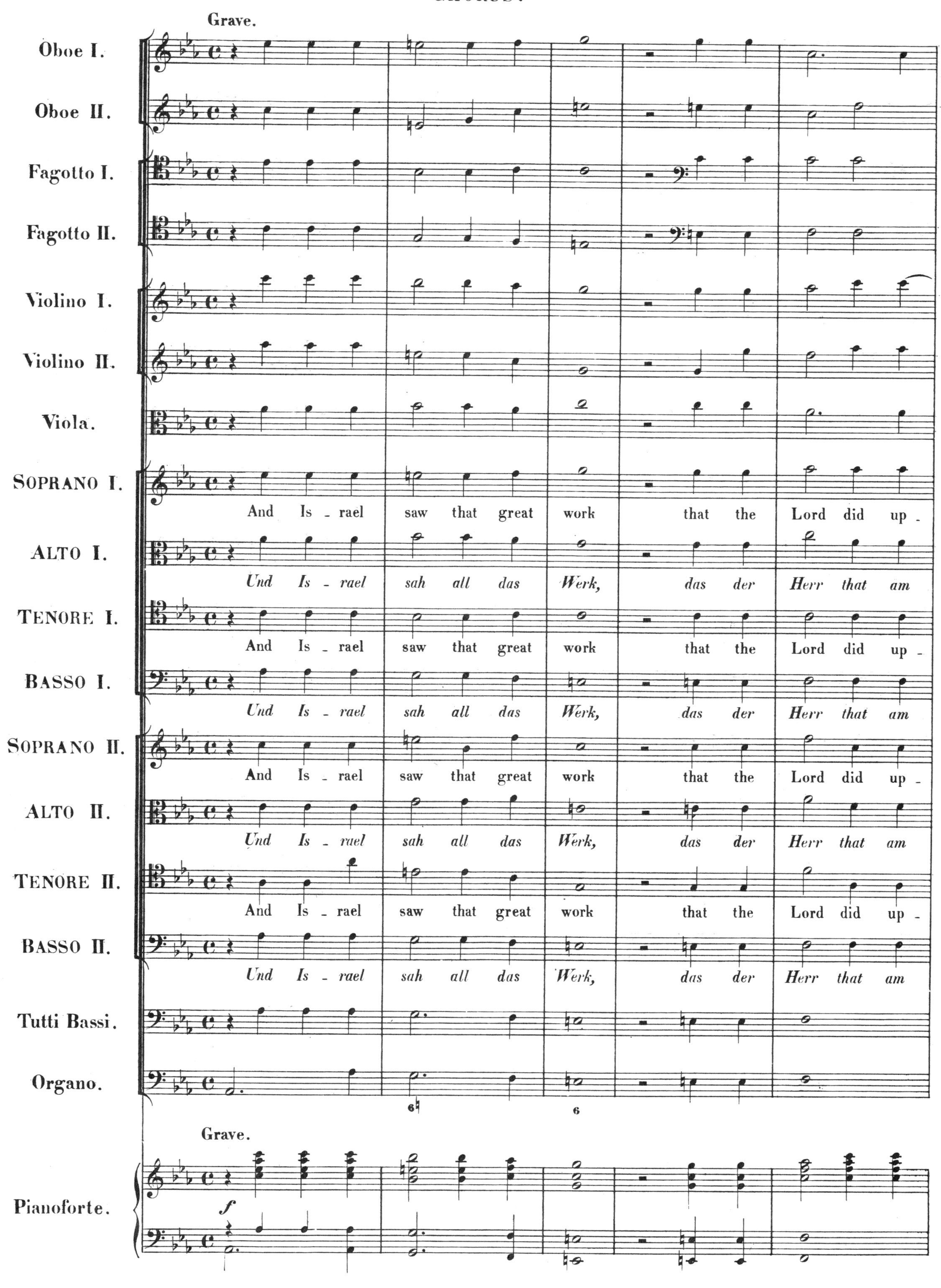
Grave.
Oboe I.
Oboe II.
Fagotto I.
Fagotto II.
Violino I.
Violino II.
Viola.
SOPRANO I.
And Is - rael saw that great work that the Lord did up -
ALTO I.
Und Is - rael sah all das Werk, das der Herr that am
TENORE I.
And Is - rael saw that great work that the Lord did up -
BASSO I.
Und Is - rael sah all das Werk, das der Herr that am
SOPRANO II.
And Is - rael saw that great work that the Lord did up -
ALTO II.
Und Is - rael sah all das Werk, das der Herr that am
TENORE II.
And Is - rael saw that great work that the Lord did up -
BASSO II.
Und Is - rael sah all das Werk, das der Herr that am
Tutti Bassi.
Organo.
Grave.
Pianoforte.

on th'E - gyp - tians; and the peo - ple fear - ed the Lord.
Land Ae - gyp - ten; und ganz Is - rael fürch - te - te ihn.
on th'E - gyp - tians; and the peo - ple fear - ed the Lord.
Land Ae - gyp - ten; und ganz Is - rael fürch - te - te ihn.
on th'E - gyp - tians; and the peo - ple fear - ed the Lord.
Land Ae - gyp - ten; und ganz Is - rael fürch - te - te ihn.
on th'E - gyp - tians; and the peo - ple fear - ed the Lord.
Land Ae - gyp - ten; und ganz Is - rael fürch - te - te ihn.

Larghetto.
Oboe I.II.
Fagotti.
Violino I.II.
Viola.
SOPRANO.
ALTO.
TENORE.
BASSO.
Tutti Bassi.
Tasto solo.
Pianoforte.
And be - lieved the Lord and his servant Moses, his servant Moses,
Und er - kann - te den Herrn und sei - nen Die - ner Mo - ses, sei - nen Die - ner Mo - ses,
and his servant Moses,
und sei - nen Die - ner Mo - ses,
unis.
and be - lieved the Lord and his
und er - kann - te den Herrn und sei - nen

ser - - vant, his ser - - vant, his ser - - vant Mo - ses; and the
Die - - ner, sei_nen Die - - ner, sei_nen Die - - ner Mo - ses;
liev_ed the Lord and his ser - vant Mo - ses, his ser - - vant Mo - ses; und ganz
kann_te den Herrn und sei_nen Die - ner Mo - ses, sei_nen Die - - ner Mo - ses;
and be - liev_ed the Lord and his ser - - vant Mo - ses; and the
und er - kann_te den Herrn und sei_nen Die - - ner Mo - ses;
and be - liev_ed the Lord and his ser - vant Mo - ses; und ganz
und er - kann_te den Herrn und den Die - ner Mo - ses;
peo_ple fear_ed the Lord, and be - liev_ed the Lord and his ser - vant Mo -
Is - rael fürch_te_te ihn, und er - kann_te den Herrn und sei_nen Die - ner Mo -
peo_ple fear_ed the Lord, and be - liev_ed the Lord and his ser - vant Mo -
Is - rael fürch_te_te ihn, und er - kann_te den Herrn und sei_nen Die - ner Mo -

ses, and be - liev-ed the Lord and his ser - vant Mo - ses, his servant Mo -
ses, und er - kann-te den Herrn und sei-nen Die - ner Mo - ses, sei-nen Die-ner Mo -
ses, and be - liev-ed the Lord and his ser - vant Mo-ses, his ser -
und er - kann-te den Herrn und sei-nen Die - ner Mo-ses, sei-nen Die -
ses, and be - liev - ed the Lord and his ser - vant
und er - kann - te den Herrn und sei-nen Die - ner
ses, and be - liev-ed the
und er - kann-te den
ses, and be - liev-ed the Lord, the Lord and his ser - vant Mo - ses; and the
ses, und er - kann-te den Herrn, den Herrn und sei-nen Die - ner Mo - ses; und ganz
vant, his ser - vant Mo - ses;
ner, sei-nen Die - ner Mo - ses;
Mo - ses, be - liev-ed the Lord and his ser - vant Mo - ses; and the peo - ple
Mo - ses, er - kann-te den Herrn und sei-nen Die - ner Mo - ses; und ganz Is - ra - el
Lord and his ser - vant Mo - ses, his ser - vant Mo - ses;
Herrn und sei-nen Die - ner Mo - ses, sei-nen Die - ner Mo - ses;

peo - ple fear - ed the Lord, and the peo - ple fear - ed the Lord, and be - liev - ed the Lord, be -
Is - ra - el fürch - te - te ihn, und ganz Is - rael fürch - te - te ihn, und er - kann - te den Herrn, er -
and the peo - ple fear - ed, fear - ed the Lord, and be -
und ganz Is - ra - el fürchtet, fürch - te - te ihn, und er -
fear - ed the Lord, and the peo - ple fear - ed, fear - ed the Lord, and be -
fürch - te - te ihn, und ganz Is - rael fürch - tet, fürch - te - te ihn, und er -
and the peo - ple fear - ed the Lord, and be -
und ganz Is - ra - el fürch - te - te ihn, und er -
liev - ed the Lord and his servant Mo - ses.
kann - te den Herrn und sei - nen Die - ner Mo - ses.
liev - ed the Lord and his ser - vant Mo - ses.
kann - te den Herrn und sei - nen Die - ner Mo - ses.
liev - ed the Lord and his ser - vant Mo - ses.
kann - te den Herrn und sei - nen Die - ner Mo - ses.
liev - ed the Lord and his ser - vant Mo - ses.
kann - te den Herrn und sei - nen Die - ner Mo - ses.
mp

Moses' Song.
Moses' Gesang.

Introitus.

tr
tr
tr
Mo
Mo
Mo
Mo
Mo
Mo
Mo
Mo
tr
ff

ses, and the chil - dren of Is - rael sung this song un -
ses und die Kin - der von Is - rael san-gen al - so
ses, and the chil - dren of Is - rael sung this song un -
ses und die Kin - der von Is - rael san-gen al - so
ses, and the chil - dren of Is - rael sung this song un -
ses und die Kin - der von Is - rael san-gen al - so
ses, and the chil - dren of Is - rael sung this song un -
ses und die Kin - der von Is - rael san-gen al - so

to the Lord, and spake say - - - ing:
zu dem Herrn, ihn laut prei - - - send:
to the Lord, and spake say - - - ing:
zu dem Herrn, ihn laut prei - - - send:
to the Lord, and spake say - - - ing:
zu dem Herrn, ihn laut prei - - - send:
to the Lord, and spake say - - - ing:
zu dem Herrn, ihn laut prei - - - send:

CHORUS.

A tempo giusto.
I will sing unto the Lord, for he hath triumphed glo-
Ich will singen zu dem Herrn, denn er hat geholfen wun-
I will sing unto the Lord, for he hath triumphed glo-
Ich will singen zu dem Herrn, denn er hat geholfen wun-
for he hath triumphed glo-
denn er hat geholfen wun-
for he hath triumphed glo-
denn er hat geholfen wun-
Tasto solo.
A tempo giusto.
f

for he hath triumphed glo - riously,
denn er hat ge-holfen wun - derbar,
riously, glo-riously, gloriously,
derbar, wun-derbar, wunderbar,
riously, glo-riously, glo-riously, gloriously,
derbar, wun-derbar, wun-derbar, wunderbar,
for he hath triumphed glo - riously,
denn er hat ge-hol-fen wun - derbar,
for he hath triumphed
denn er hat ge-hol-fen
riously, for he hath triumphed
der-bar, denn er hat ge-hol-fen
riously, for he hath triumphed
der-bar, denn er hat ge-hol-fen
for he
denn er

for he hath triumphed
denn er hat ge-hol-fen
for he
denn er
gloriously, glo - - - riously, glo - - - riously, glo - - - - - - - riously,
wun-derbar, wun - - - derbar, wun - - - derbar, wun - - - - - - - derbar,
glo - - - riously, glo - - - riously, glo - - - riously, he hath tri-umphed gloriously,
wun - - - derbar, wun - - - derbar, wun - - - der-bar, er hat ge-holfen wunderbar,
gloriously, gloriously, gloriously, glo-riously, glo-riously, gloriously, he hath tri-umphed gloriously,
wun-derbar, wun-derbar, wunderbar, wun-derbar, wun-derbar, wunder-bar, er hat ge-holfen wunderbar,
hath triumphed glo - - - riously, gloriously,
hat ge-holfen wun - - - derbar, wunderbar,

glo
wun
riously,
der_bar,
hath triumphed glo
hat ge_hol_fen wun
riously,
der_bar,
the horse and his ri_der
das Ross und den Rei_ter
the horse and his ri_der hath he
das Ross und den Rei_ter hat ge_

I will sing unto the
ich will sin - gen zu dem
I will sing, the horse and his ri-der hath he thrown in-to the
ich will sin-gen, das Ross und den Rei-ter hat ge-stürzt er in das
the horse and his ri-der, the horse and his ri-der hath he thrown in-to the
das Ross und den Rei-ter, das Ross und den Rei-ter hat ge-stürzt er in das
hath he thrown in-to the sea;
hat ge-stürzt er in das Meer,
thrown in-to the sea,
stürzt er in das Meer;

Lord, un - - - to the Lord,
Herrn, zu dem Herrn,
sea, in - to the sea,
Meer, ge-stürzt in's Meer,
sea, in - to the sea,
Meer, ge-stürzt in's Meer,
I will sing
ich will sin - - - - - - - - - - - -
the horse, the horse and his ri - der, the horse and his ri - der
das Ross, das Ross und den Rei-ter, das Ross und den Rei-ter
the horse and his ri - der, the horse and his ri - der, the horse and his ri - der
das Ross und den Rei-ter, das Ross und den Rei-ter, das Ross und den Rei-ter
I will sing
ich will sin - - - - - - - - - - - -

he
er
hath triumphed glo - - - - riously,
hat ge-hol-fen wun - - - - derbar,
he
er
hath triumphed glo-riously,
hat ge-hol-fen wun-der-bar,
glo-riously,
wun-derbar,
gloriously,
wunderbar,
he hath triumphed
er hat ge-hol-fen
glo-riously,
wun-derbar,
gloriously,
wunderbar,
he hath triumphed
er hat ge-hol-fen
glo - - - - riously,
wun - - - - derbar,
un-to the Lord,
gen zu dem Herrn,
he
er
hath he thrown in-to the sea,
hat gestürzt er in das Meer,
he hath triumphed
er hat ge-holfen
hath he thrown in-to the sea,
hat gestürzt er in das Meer,
he hath triumphed
er hat ge-holfen
un-to the Lord,
gen zu dem Herrn,
he
er
6 7

the horse and his ri - der
das Ross und den Rei - ter
the horse and his ri - der hath he
das Ross und den Rei - ter hat ge -
the horse and his ri - der
das Ross und den Rei - ter
the horse and his ri - der hath he
das Ross und den Rei - ter hat ge -
hath triumphed glo - riously, he hath tri - umphed gloriously,
hat ge - hol - fen wun - der - bar, er hat ge - hol - fen wun - derbar,
glo - riously;
wun - der - bar;
glo - riously;
wun - der - bar;
hath triumphed glo - riously,
hat ge - hol - fen wun - der - bar,

hath he thrown in - to the sea;
hat ge-stürzt er in das Meer;
thrown in - to the sea.
stürzt er in das Meer,
hath he thrown in - to the sea,
hat ge-stürzt er in das Meer,
thrown in - to the sea;
stürzt er in das Meer;
the horse and his ri-der, the horse and his ri-der hath he thrown in - to the
das Ross und den Rei-ter, das Ross und den Rei-ter hat ge-stürzt er in das
I will sing un - to the
ich will sin - gen zu dem
I will sing un - to the
ich will sin - gen zu dem
the horse and his ri-der, the horse and his ri-der hath he thrown in - to the
das Ross und den Rei-ter, das Ross und den Rei-ter hat ge-stürzt er in das

I will
ich will
sing
sin
the horse and his ri-der, the
das Ross und den Rei-ter, das
horse and his ri-der, the horse and his ri-der hath
Ross und den Rei-ter, das Ross und den Rei-ter hat
the
das
horse and his ri-der, the horse and his ri-der
Ross und den Rei-ter, das Ross und den Rei-ter
I will
ich will
sing
sin
sea, in-to the sea,
Meer, ge-stürzt ins Meer,
Lord, un-to the Lord,
Her - ren, zu dem Herrn,
Lord, un-to the Lord,
Her - ren, zu dem Herrn,
sea, in-to the sea,
Meer, ge-stürzt ins Meer,

un - to the Lord, un - to the Lord, he
- gen zu dem Her - ren, zu dem Herrn, er
he thrown in - to the sea, hath he thrown in - to the sea,
er gestürzt in das Meer, hat ge - stürzt er in das Meer,
hath he thrown in - to the sea. in - to the sea, he
hat ge - stürzt er in das Meer, ge - stürzt in's Meer, er
un - to the Lord,
- gen zu dem Herrn,
he hath triumphed glo - - -
er hat ge - holfen wun - - -
he hath triumphed glo - riously, glo - riously,
er hat ge - holfen wun - derbar, wun - der - bar,
he hath triumphed glo - riously, glo - riously,
er hat ge - holfen wun - derbar, wun - der - bar,
he hath triumphed glo - - -
er hat ge - holfen wun - - -

hath triumphed glo - riously, the horse and his ri-der, the horse
hat ge-holfen wun - derbar,
he hath triumphed glo-riously, glo-riously, gloriously, das Ross und den Reiter, das Ross
er hat ge-hol-fen wun-derbar, wun-derbar, wunderbar,
hath triumphed glo-riously, glo-riously, gloriously, the horse and his ri-der, the horse
hat ge-holfen wun-derbar, wun-derbar, wunderbar,
he hath triumphed glo - riously, das Ross und den Reiter, das Ross
er hat ge-hol-fen wun - derbar,
- riously, the horse and his ri-der, the horse and his
- derbar,
gloriously, das Ross und den Reiter, das Ross und den
wunderbar,
gloriously, the horse and his ri-der, the horse and his
wunderbar,
- riously, das Ross und den Reiter, das Ross und den
- derbar,

and his ri - der hath he thrown in - to the sea, the horse and his ri - der, the
und den Reiter hat gestürzt er in das Meer, das Ross und den Reiter, das
and his ri - der hath he thrown in - to the sea, the horse and his ri - der, the
und den Reiter hat gestürzt er in das Meer, das Ross und den Reiter, das
ri - der hath he thrown, hath he thrown in - to the sea, the horse and his ri - der, the
Rei - ter hat gestürzt, hat ge - stürzt er in das Meer, das Ross und den Reiter, das
ri - der hath he thrown, hath he thrown in - to the sea, the horse and his ri - der, the
Rei - ter hat gestürzt, hat ge - stürzt er in das Meer, das Ross und den Reiter, das
ff

horse and his ri-der, the horse and his ri-der, the horse and his ri-der hath he thrown in-to the sea, the
Ross und den Rei-ter, das Ross und den Reiter, das Ross und den Reiter hat er ge-stürzt in das Meer, das
horse and his ri-der, the horse and his ri-der, the horse and his ri-der hath he thrown in-to the sea, the
Ross und den Rei-ter, das Ross und den Reiter, das Ross und den Reiter hat er ge-stürzt in das Meer, das
horse and his ri-der, the horse and his ri-der, the horse and his ri-der hath he thrown in-to the sea, the
Ross und den Rei-ter, das Ross und den Reiter, das Ross und den Reiter hat er ge-stürzt in das Meer, das
horse and his ri-der, the horse and his ri-der, the horse and his ri-der hath he thrown in-to the sea, the
Ross und den Rei-ter, das Ross und den Reiter, das Ross und den Reiter hat er ge-stürzt in das Meer, das

horse and his ri_der, the horse and his ri_der hath
he thrown in_to the sea;
Ross und den Rei_ter, das Ross und den Rei_ter hat
er ge_stürzt in das Meer;
horse and his ri_der, the horse and his ri_der hath
he thrown in_to the sea;
Ross und den Rei_ter, das Ross und den Rei_ter hat
er ge_stürzt in das Meer;
I
will
ich
will
horse and his ri_der, the horse and his ri_der hath
he thrown in_to the sea;
Ross und den Rei_ter, das Ross und den Rei_ter hat
er ge_stürzt in das Meer;
horse and his ri_der, the horse and his ri_der hath
he thrown in_to the sea;
Ross und den Rei_ter, das Ross und den Rei_ter hat
er ge_stürzt in das Meer;
I
will
ich
will
mf

I will sing unto the Lord, for he
ich will singen zu dem Herrn, denn er
I will sing unto the Lord, for he hath triumphed
ich will singen zu dem Herrn, denn er hat geholfen
I will sing unto the Lord,
ich will singen zu dem Herrn,
sing unto the Lord, for he
singen zu dem Herrn, denn er
I will sing unto the Lord, for he
ich will singen zu dem Herrn, denn er
I will sing unto the Lord, for he hath triumphed
ich will singen zu dem Herrn, denn er hat geholfen
I will sing unto the Lord,
ich will singen zu dem Herrn,
sing unto the Lord, for he
singen zu dem Herrn, denn er

hath triumphed glo - - - - - - - - - - - - riously, he hath triumphed glo - riously, the
hat ge-hol-fen wun - - - - - - - - - - - der-bar, er hat ge-hol-fen wun - der-bar, das
glo - - - - - - riously, glo - riously, glo - riously, er hat ge-hol-fen wun - der-bar, das
wun - - - - - der-bar, wun - der-bar, wun - der-bar,
for he hath tri - umphed glo-rious - ly, glo - riously, he hath triumphed glo - riously, the
denn er hat ge - hol-fen wun-der - bar, wun - der-bar,
hath triumphed glo - - - - - - - - - - - - riously, er hat ge-hol-fen wun - der-bar, das
hat ge-hol-fen wun - - - - - - - - - - - der-bar,
ff

horse and his ri_der hath he thrown in_to the sea, the horse and his ri_der, the horse and his ri_der hath
Ross und den Reiter hat er ge_stürzt in das Meer, das Ross und den Rei_ter, das Ross und den Rei_ter hat
horse and his ri_der hath he thrown in_to the sea, the horse and his ri_der, the horse and his ri_der hath
Ross und den Reiter hat er ge_stürzt in das Meer, das Ross und den Rei_ter, das Ross und den Rei_ter hat
horse and his ri_der hath he thrown in_to the sea, the horse and his ri_der, the horse and his ri_der hath
Ross und den Reiter hat er ge_stürzt in das Meer, das Ross und den Rei_ter, das Ross und den Rei_ter hat
horse and his ri_der hath he thrown in_to the sea, the horse and his ri_der, the horse and his ri_der hath
Ross und den Reiter hat er ge_stürzt in das Meer, das Ross und den Rei_ter, das Ross und den Rei_ter hat

he thrown in-to the sea, hath he thrown in- to the sea.
er ge-stürzt in das Meer, hat er ge- stürzt in das Meer.
he thrown in-to the sea, hath he thrown in- to the sea.
er ge-stürzt in das Meer, hat er ge- stürzt in das Meer.
he thrown in-to the sea, hath he thrown in- to the sea.
er ge-stürzt in das Meer, hat er ge- stürzt in das Meer.
he thrown in-to the sea, hath he thrown in- to the sea.
er ge-stürzt in das Meer, hat er ge- stürzt in das Meer.
mp

Larghetto.
Violini unisoni.
SOPRANO I.
SOPRANO II.
Larghetto.
Pianoforte.
mf
mp
p
The Lord is my strength and my song,
Der Herr ist mein Heil und mein Lied,
The Lord is my strength and my song,
Der Herr ist mein Heil und mein Lied,
the Lord is my strength and my song, and my song,
der Herr ist mein Heil und mein Lied, und mein Lied,
the Lord is my strength and my song, and my
der Herr ist mein Heil und mein Lied, und mein

He is be- come my sal- va - - - - tion, my sal -
Er ward al- lein mein Er- lö - - - - ser, mein Er -
song, He is be- come my sal- va - - - - tion, my sal -
Lied, Er ward al - lein mein Er- lö - - - - ser, mein Er -
va- tion, my sal - va- tion, He is become my strength, my song, He is be -
lö - ser, mein Er - lö - ser, Er ward allein mein Heil, mein Lied, Er ward al -
va- tion, my sal - va- tion, He is become my sal- va- tion, my sal- va- tion,
lö - ser, mein Er - lö - ser, Er ward allein mein Er- lö- ser, mein Er- lö- ser,
come my sal- va - tion, my sal- va - tion, my sal- va- tion,
lein mein Er- lö - ser, mein Er - lö - ser, mein Er- lö- ser,
He is be- come my sal- va - tion, my sal - va - tion, my sal- va- tion, and
Er ward al- lein mein Er- lö - ser, mein Er - lö - ser, mein Er- lö - ser, ward

my sal - va - tion,
mein Er - lö - ser,
He is be - come
nur Er al - lein
my sal - vation,
mein Er - lö - ser,
my sal - va - tion,
mein Er - lö - ser,
He is be - come my
nur Er al - lein mein
strength, my
Heil, mein
my sal - va - tion,
mein Er - lö - ser,
He is be - come
Er ward al - lein
my sal - va - tion;
mein Er - lö - ser;
the
der
song,
Lied,
He is be - come
Er ward al - lein
my sal - va - tion; the
mein Er - lö - ser; der
Lord is my
Herr ist mein
Lord is my strength and my song, the
Herr ist mein Heil und mein Lied, der
Lord is my strength and my song,
Herr ist mein Heil und mein Lied,
strength and my song, the Lord is my
Heil und mein Lied, der Herr ist mein
strength and my song,
Heil und mein Lied,
He is be - come my sal -
Er ward al - lein mein Er -

He is be-come my sal-va-tion, my sal-va-tion, my sal-va-tion, He is be-
Er ward al-lein mein Er-lö-ser, mein Er-lö-ser, mein Er-lö-ser, nur Er al-
va-tion,
lö-ser,
my sal-va-tion, He is be-
mein Er-lö-ser, nur Er al-
come my sal-va-tion, He is be-
lein mein Er-lö-ser, nur Er al-
come my sal-va-tion, my sal-va-tion, He is become
lein mein Er-lö-ser, mein Er-lö-ser, nur Er al-lein
come my sal-va-tion, my sal-va-tion, my sal-
lein mein Er-lö-ser, mein Er-lö-ser, mein Er-
my sal-va-tion, my sal-va-tion, my sal-va-
mein Er-lö-ser, mein Er-lö-ser, mein Er-lö-

va - - - tion. He is be - come
lö - - - ser, nur Er al - lein
my sal - va - - - - - - - - - -
mein Er - lö - - - - - - - - - -
- - - - tion. He is be - come
- - - - ser, nur Er al - lein
mf
mp
tion, my sal - va - tion.
ser, mein Er - lö - ser.
f
Viol. I.
Viol. II.
Viola.

CHORUS.
Grave.
Trombone I.II.
Trombone III.
Oboe I.
Oboe II.
Fagotti.
Violino I.
Violino II.
Viola.
SOPRANO I.
He is my God, and I will pre - pare him an ha - bi - ta - tion, I will pre -
Er ist mein Gott, und ich will be - rei - ten ihm ei - ne Wohnung, ich will be -
ALTO I.
He is my God, and I will pre - pare him an ha - bi - ta - tion, I will pre -
Er ist mein Gott, und ich will be - rei - ten ihm ei - ne Woh - nung, ich will be -
TENORE I.
He is my God, and I will pre - pare him an ha - bi - ta - tion, I will pre -
Er ist mein Gott, und ich will be - rei - ten ihm ei - ne Woh - nung, ich will be -
BASSO I.
He is my God, and I will pre - pare him an ha - bi - ta - tion, I will pre -
Er ist mein Gott, und ich will be - rei - ten ihm ei - ne Woh - nung, ich will be -
SOPRANO II.
He is my God, and I will prepare him an ha - bi - ta - tion, and I will pre -
Er ist mein Gott, und ich will be - rei - ten ihm ei - ne Woh - nung, und ich will be -
ALTO II.
He is my God, and I will pre - pare him an ha - bi - ta - tion, I will pre -
Er ist mein Gott, und ich will be - rei - ten ihm ei - ne Woh - nung, ich will be -
TENORE II.
He is my God, and I will pre - pare him an ha - bi - ta - tion, and I will pre -
Er ist mein Gott, und ich will be - rei - ten ihm ei - ne Woh - nung, und ich will be -
BASSO II.
He is my God, and I will pre - pare him an ha - bi - ta - tion, I will pre -
Er ist mein Gott, und ich will be - rei - ten ihm ei - ne Woh - nung, ich will be -
Tutti Bassi, e Organo.
Grave.
Pianoforte.
f

pare him an ha - - - bi - ta - tion, my fa - ther's God.
rei - - - ten ihm ei - - - - ne Woh-nung, meines Va - ters Gott.
pare him, I will pre - pare him an ha - - - bi - - ta - tion, my fa-ther's God.
rei - ten, ich will be - rei - ten ihm ei - - - - ne Woh-nung, meines Va - ters Gott.
pare him, I will pre - pare him an ha - - - - bi - ta - tion, my fa - ther's God.
rei - ten, ich will be - rei - ten ihm ei - - - - - ne Woh-nung, meines Va - ters Gott.
pare him, I will pre - pare him an ha - - - - bi - ta - tion, my fa - ther's God.
rei - ten, ich will be - rei - ten ihm ei - - - - ne Woh-nung, meines Va - ters Gott.
pare him an ha - - - - bi - ta - tion, my fa - ther's God.
rei - - - - - - ten ihm ei - - - - ne Woh-nung, meines Va - ters Gott.
pare, pre - pare him an ha - - - - bi - ta - tion, my fa - ther's God.
rei - ten, be - rei - ten ihm ei - - - - ne Woh-nung, meines Va - ters Gott.
pare him, I will pre - pare him an ha - - - - bi - ta - tion, my fa-ther's God.
rei - ten, ich will be - rei - ten ihm ei - - - - - ne Woh-nung, meines Va - ters Gott.
pare him an ha - - - - bi - ta - tion, my fa - ther's God.
rei - - - - - - ten ihm ei - - - - ne Woh-nung, meines Va - ters Gott.

SOPRANO.
And I will ex - alt him,
Und ich will ihn prei - sen,
ALTO.
And I will ex - alt him,
Und ich will ihn prei - sen,
TENORE.
And I will ex - alt him, I
Und ich will ihn prei - sen, ich
BASSO.
And I will ex - alt him, I will ex-
Und ich will ihn prei - sen, ich will ihn
Continuo.
Organo tasto solo, senza Violonc. e Fagotti.
mf
I will ex - alt
ich will ihn prei -
will ex - alt him, I will ex - alt him, I will ex-
will ihn prei - sen, ich will ihn prei - sen, ich will ihn
alt him, I will ex - alt him,
prei - sen, ich will ihn prei - sen,

Trombone I.
Trombone II.
Trombone III.
Oboe I.
Oboe II.
Violino I.
Violino II.
Viola.
I will ex-alt him, I will ex-alt him,
ich will ihn prei-sen, ich will ihn prei-sen,
him, I will ex-alt, I will ex-alt him, I will ex-
sen, ich will ihn preisen, ich will ihn prei-sen, ich will ihn
alt him, and I will ex-alt him, I will ex-alt
prei-sen, und ich will ihn prei-sen, ich will ihn prei-
and I will ex-alt him,
und ich will ihn prei-sen,
Tutti Bassi.
6
f

and I will ex - alt him, I will ex-alt him, I will ex-alt him;
und ich will ihn prei - - sen, ich will ihn prei - sen, ich will ihn prei - sen,
alt him, I will ex-alt him, I will ex-alt him;
prei - - - - - - - - sen, ich will ihn prei - sen, ich will ihn prei - sen,
him, I will ex-alt him, I will ex-alt him;
sen, ich will ihn prei - sen, ich will ihn prei - - - sen,
I will ex - alt, I will ex-alt him, I will ex - alt, I will ex-alt him;
ich will ihn preisen, ich will ihn prei - sen, ich will ihn preisen, ich will ihn prei - sen,
mp

He is my fa-ther's God, He is my fa-ther's God, I will ex-alt, I will ex-alt him, ex-
Ihn, meines Va-ters Gott, Ihn, mei - nes Va-ters Gott, ich will ihn preisen, ich will ihn prei-sen, ihn
He is my fa-ther's God, He is my father's God, and I will ex-alt
Ihn, meines Va-ters Gott, Ihn, meines Va-ters Gott, und ich will ihn prei
He is my fa-ther's God, He is my fa-ther's God,
Ihn, meines Va-ters Gott, Ihn, meines Va-ters Gott,
He is my fa-ther's God, He is my fa-ther's God, I
Ihn, meines Va-ters Gott, Ihn, meines Va-ters Gott, ich
f
cresc.
ff
mp

alt him, I, I will ex-alt him, and
prei - sen, ich, ich will ihn prei - sen, und
him, I will ex - alt him,
sen, ich will ihn prei - sen,
I will ex - alt, I will ex-alt him,
ich will ihn preisen, ich will ihn prei - sen,
will ex - alt, I will ex-alt him, and I will ex - alt him, I
will ihn preisen, ich will ihn prei - sen, und ich will ihn prei - sen, ich
Tutti.
mf

I
will ex - alt
him,
and
I
will,
I
will
ex - alt
ich
will ihn
prei -
sen,
und
ich
will,
ich
will
ihn
prei
I
will ex - alt
him, ex - alt
ich
will ihn
prei
sen, ihn
prei
I
will ex - alt
ich
will ihn
prei
will ex - alt
him,
I
will
ex - alt
will ihn
prei
sen,
ich
will
ihn
prei
f

him, I, I will ex - alt him, I, I will ex - alt him,
sen, ich, ich will ihn prei - sen, ich, ich will ihn prei - sen,
him, I will ex - alt him, I, I will ex - alt him, I will ex - alt him, I
sen, ich will ihn prei - sen, ich, ich will ihn prei - sen, ich will ihn prei - sen, ich
him, I will ex - alt him, I will ex - alt him, I, I
sen, ich will ihn prei - sen, ich will ihn prei - sen, ich, ich
him, I, I, I will ex - alt him, I will ex - alt
sen, ich, ich, ich will ihn prei - sen, ich will ihn prei -

I will ex-alt him, I will ex-alt him.
ich will ihn prei sen, ich will ihn prei sen.
will ex-alt him, I, I will ex alt him, I will ex alt him.
will ihn preisen, ich, ich will ihn prei sen, ich will ihn prei sen.
will ex-alt him, I will ex-alt him, I will ex alt him, I will ex alt him.
will ihn preisen, ich will ihn prei sen, ich will ihn prei sen, ich will ihn prei sen.
him, I will ex- alt him.
sen, ich will ihn prei sen.

Andante allegro.
Oboe I.II.
Fagotti.
Violino I.
Violino II.
Viola.
BASSO I.
BASSO II.
Organo, e Bassi.
Andante allegro.
Pianoforte.

tr
tr
mf

The
Der
ritard.
cresc.
f
mezzo piano
Lord is a man of war, the Lord, the Lord is a man of war,
Herr ist der star-ke Held, der Herr, der Herr ist der star-ke Held,
a tempo.
mp
mf

the
Lord is a man of
war,
der
Herr ist der star_ke
Held,
The
Lord is a man of
war,
Der
Herr ist der star_ke
Held,
mp
the
Lord is a man of
war,
der
Herr ist der star_ke
Held,
the
Lord, the
Lord is a man of
der
Herr, der
Herr ist der starke

war,
Held,
Lord
Herr
is his
ist sein
name,
Nam',
is his
ist sein
name,
Nam',
Lord,
Herr,
Lord is his
Herr ist sein
name,
Nam',
is his
ist sein
name,
Nam',
Lord is his
Herr ist sein
name,
Nam',
is his
ist sein
name,
Nam',
Lord is his
Herr ist sein
name,
Nam',

Lord is his
Herr ist sein
name,
Nam',
is his
ist sein
name,
Nam',
Lord is his
Herr ist sein
name,
Nam',
is his
ist sein
name,
Nam',
Lord is his
Herr ist sein
name,
Nam',
Lord is his
Herr ist sein
name,
Nam',
Lord
Herr
Lord
Herr
is his
ist sein
name;
Nam';
Pha - raoh's
Pha - ra - o's
chariots,
Wa - gen
is his
ist sein
name;
Nam';
Pha - raoh's
Pha - ra - o's
chariots,
Wa - gen
and his
und sein

and his host,
und sein Heer
hath he cast in-to the sea, hath he
hat er in das Meer ge-stürzt, hat ge-
host, hath he cast in-to the sea, hath he cast
Heer hat er in das Meer ge-stürzt, hat ge-stürzt
cast in-to the sea.
stürzt er in das Meer.
in-to the sea.
er in das Meer.

The
Der
Lord is a man of
Herr ist der star-ke
war,
Held,
The
Der
(p)
mp
p
Lord is a man of
Herr ist der star-ke
war,
Held,
Lord is his name;
Herr ist sein Nam';

Pha_ra_oh's
chariots,
and his
host,
hath he
cast in _ to the
Pha_ra_o's
Wa_gen
und sein
Heer
hat ge -
stürzt er in das
Lord is his
name;
Herr ist sein
Nam';
Pha _ ra_oh's
chariots,
and his
host,
Pha _ ra_o's
Wa_gen
und sein
Heer
forte
mf
sea,
Meer,
hath he
cast
hat ge -
stürzt
hath he
cast in _ to the
sea,
hath
he
cast
hat ge -
stürzt er in das
Meer,
hat
ge -
- stürzt

into the sea.
er in das Meer.
into the sea.
er in das Meer.
ritard.
a tempo.
cresc.

His chosen captains also are
All' seine Helden, alle ver-
His chosen captains
All' seine Helden,
drowned, also are drowned,
sanken, alle ver- sanken,
are drown - - - - - - -
ver- san - - - - - - -
also are drowned, also are drowned,
alle ver- sanken, alle ver- sanken,
are drown - -
ver- san - - -

- ed, are drown - - - ed in the Red sea, his cho-sen captains al-so are
- ken, ver - san - - - ken in dem Schilf-meer, all' sei-ne Hel-den, al-le ver-
- - - - - - - - ed in the Red sea, his cho-sen cap-tains
- - - - - - - - ken in dem Schilf-meer, all' sei-ne Hel-den,
drowned, al-so are drowned, al-so are drowned, his chosen
san-ken, al-le ver-san-ken, al-le ver-san-ken, all' sei-ne
al-so are drowned, al-so are drowned, his chosen
al-le ver-san-ken, al-le ver-san-ken, all' sei-ne

captains also are drowned, also are drowned in the Red sea,
Hel-den al-le ver-san-ken, al-le ver-san-ken in dem Schilf-meer,
captains also are drowned, also are drowned in the Red sea, al-so are
Hel-den al-le ver-san-ken, al-le ver-san-ken in dem Schilf-meer, al-le ver-
tempo ad libit.
a tempo.
mp
al-so are drown-ed in the Red
al-le ver-san-ken in dem Schilf-
drown-ed, al-so are drown, ed in the Red
san-ken, al-le ver-san-ken in dem Schilf-

sea,
his cho-sen
cap-tains
al-so are
drowned,
al-so are
drowned in
the Red
sea.
meer,
all' sei-ne
Hel-den,
al-le ver-
san-ken,
al-le ver-
san-ken in
dem Schilf-
meer.
sea,
his cho-sen
cap-tains
al-so are
drowned,
al-so are
drowned in
the Red
sea.
meer,
all' sei-ne
Hel-den,
al-le ver-
san-ken,
al-le ver-
san-ken in
dem Schilf-
meer.
tempo ad libit.
ritard.
a tempo.

p
mf

tr
tr
ritard.
cresc.
f

CHORUS.

Largo.
Oboe I.
Oboe II.
Fagotti.
Violino I.
Violino II.
Viola.
SOPRANO I.
The
Die
ALTO I.
TENORE I.
The depths have co_ver'd them, the depths have cover'd them,
Die Tie_fe deckte sie, die Tie_fe deckte sie,
BASSO I.
The depths have cover'd them,
Die Tie_ _fe deckte sie,
SOPRANO II.
ALTO II.
The depths have co_ver'd them, the depths have cover'd them,
Die Tie_fe deckte sie, die Tie_fe deckte sie,
TENORE II.
The depths have co_ver'd them, the depths have cover'd them.
Die Tie_fe deckte sie, die Tie_fe deckte sie,
BASSO II.
The depths have cover'd them,
Die Tie_ _fe deckte sie,
Tutti Bassi, e Cembalo.
Organo.
Piano, tasto solo e l'ottava.
Largo.
Pianoforte.

depths have cover'd them, the depths have cover'd them, they sank in-to the
Tie - fe deckte sie, die Tie-fe deckte sie, sie sanken hin-ab zum
The depths have cover'd them, the depths have co - ver'd them, they sank, they sank in-to the
Die Tie-fe deckte sie, die Tie-fe deck - te sie, sie sanken, sie sanken in den
the depths have cover'd them, the depths have co - ver'd them, they sank, they sank in-to the
die Tie-fe deckte sie, die Tie-fe deck - te sie, sie sanken, sie sanken in den
the depths have cover'd them, the depths have cover'd them, they sank in-to the
die Tie-fe deckte sie, die Tie-fe deckte sie, sie sanken hin-ab zum
The depths have cover'd them, the depths have cover'd them, they sank in-to the
die Tie-fe deckte sie, die Tie-fe deckte sie, sie sanken hin-ab zum
the depths have cover'd them, the depths have cover'd them, they sank in-to the
die Tie-fe deckte sie, die Tie-fe deckte sie, sie sanken hin-ab zum

bot_tom, they sank in_ to the bottom, in_to the bottom as a stone, the depths have
Ab_grund, sie sanken in den Abgrund, hinab zum Abgrund wie ein Stein, die Tie_fe
bot_tom, they sank in_ to the bottom, in_to the bottom as a stone, the depths have
Ab_grund, sie sanken in den Abgrund, hinab zum Abgrund wie ein Stein, die Tie_fe
bot_tom, they sank in_ to the bot_tom as a stone, as a stone, the depths have cover'd them,
Ab_grund, sie sanken in den Abgrund wie ein Stein, wie ein Stein, die Tie_fe deckte sie,
bot_tom, they sank in_ to the bot_tom as a stone, the depths have cover'd them,
Ab_grund, sie sanken in den Abgrund wie ein Stein, die Tie_fe deckte sie,

co-ver'd them, they sank in - to the bot-tom as a stone.
deck-te sie, sie san-ken in den Abgrund wie ein Stein.
co-ver'd them, they sank in - to the bot-tom as a stone.
deck-te sie, sie san-ken in den Abgrund wie ein Stein.
they sank in-to the bot-tom as a stone.
sie sanken in den Abgrund wie ein Stein.
they sank in-to the bot-tom as a stone.
sie sanken in den Abgrund wie ein Stein.
pp

CHORUS.

Andante.
Trombone I.II.
Trombone III.
Tromba I.II.
Timpani.
Oboe I.
Oboe II.
Fagotti.
Violino I.
Violino II.
Viola.
SOPRANO I.
is become glo - rious, thy right hand, oh Lord, is be_come
ALTO I.
thut gro_sse Wun - der, o Herr, dei_ne Hand thut gro_sse
TENORE I.
is become glo - rious, thy right hand, oh Lord, is be_come
BASSO I.
thut gro_sse Wun - der, o Herr, dei_ne Hand thut gro_sse
SOPRANO II.
Thy right hand, oh Lord, is become glo_rious, glo - rious, is be_come
ALTO II.
O Herr, dei_ne Hand thut gro_sse Wun_der, Wun - der, thut gro_sse
TENORE II.
Thy right hand, oh Lord, is become glo_rious, glo - rious, is be_come
BASSO II.
O Herr, dei_ne Hand thut gro_sse Wun_der, Wun - der, thut gro_sse
Tutti Bassi, e Cembalo.
Organo.
Andante con moto.
Pianoforte.
f

glo - rious in power, oh Lord, thy right hand, oh Lord, is become glorious in pow_er,
herr - li - che Wunder, o Herr, o Herr, dei_ne Hand thut gro_sse herr_li_che Wunder,
glo - rious in power, oh Lord, thy right hand, oh Lord, is become glorious in pow_er,
herr - li - che Wunder, o Herr, o Herr, dei_ne Hand thut gro_sse herr_li_che Wunder,
glo - rious in power, thy right hand, oh Lord, thy right hand, oh Lord, is become glorious in pow_er,
herr - li - che Wunder, o Herr, dei_ne Hand, o Herr, dei_ne Hand thut gro_sse herr_li_che Wunder,
glo - rious in power, thy right hand, oh Lord, thy right hand, oh Lord, is become glorious in pow_er,
herr - li - che Wunder, o Herr, dei_ne Hand, o Herr, dei_ne Hand thut gro_sse herr_li_che Wunder,
p
cresc.
f

thy right hand, oh Lord, is become glorious, glo - rious, is become glo - rious in
o Herr, dei-ne Hand thut gro-sse Wunder, Wun - der, thut gro-sse herr - li - che
thy right hand, oh Lord, is become glorious, glo - rious, is become glo - rious in
o Herr, dei-ne Hand thut gro-sse Wunder, Wun - der, thut gro-sse herr - li - che
is become glo - rious, thy right hand, oh Lord, is become glo - rious in
thut gro-sse Wun - der, o Herr, dei-ne Hand thut gro-sse herr - li - che
is become glo - rious, thy right hand, oh Lord, is become glo - rious in
thut gro-sse Wun - der, o Herr, dei-ne Hand thut gro-sse herr - li - che

power, thy right hand, oh Lord, thy right hand, oh Lord, is become glorious in pow_er:
Wun_der, o Herr, dei_ne Hand, o Herr, dei_ne Hand thut grosse herr_li_che Wunder:
power, thy right hand, oh Lord, thy right hand, oh Lord, is become glorious in pow_er:
thy right hand, oh Lord, hath dashed in
dein Arm hat, o Herr, zerschlagen in
Wun_der, o Herr, dei_ne Hand, o Herr, dei_ne Hand thut grosse herr_li_che Wunder:
power, oh Lord, thy right hand, oh Lord, is become glorious in pow_er:
Wunder, o Herr, o Herr, dei_ne Hand thut grosse herr_li_che Wunder:
power, oh Lord, thy right hand, oh Lord, is become glorious in pow_er:
Wunder, o Herr, o Herr, dei_ne Hand thut grosse herr_li_che Wunder:
Tasto solo.
p
cresc.
f
fp

thy right hand, oh Lord, hath dashed in pie_ces the e - - - ne - - my, thy right hand, oh Lord, hath dashed in
dein Arm hat, o Herr; zerschlagen in Stücke die Fein - - - des - macht, dein Arm hat, o Herr; zer_schlagen in
thy right hand, oh Lord, hath dashed in pieces the e_ne - my,
dein Arm hat, o Herr; zer - schlagen in Stücke die Fein_des - macht,
pie_ces the e - - - - - ne - my, thy right hand hath dashed in pieces, hath dashed in pie_ces the e_ne -
Stü_cke die Fein - - - - des_macht, dein Arm hat zerschlagen in Stücke, zerschlagen in Stü_cke die Feindes -
thy right hand, oh Lord, hath dash_ed in pieces the e - - - ne - -
dein Arm hat, o Herr; zer - schlagen in Stücke die Fein - - - des -
thy right hand, oh Lord, hath dash_ed in pieces, thy right hand, oh Lord, hath dashed in
dein Arm hat, o Herr; zer - schlagen in Stücke, dein Arm hat, o Herr; zer_schlagen in
thy right hand, oh Lord, hath dash_ed in pieces the e - ne - my,
dein Arm hat, o Herr; zer - schlagen in Stücke die Fein_des - macht,
thy right hand, oh Lord, hath dash_ed in pieces, hath dashed in pie_ces the e - ne -
dein Arm hat, o Herr; zer - schlagen in Stücke, zerschlagen in Stü_cke die Feindes -
thy right hand, oh Lord, hath dash_ed in pieces the e - - - ne - -
dein Arm hat, o Herr; zer - schlagen in Stücke die Fein - - - des -
Tutti.

pieces
Stü_cke
the e - - ne - my, thy right hand, oh Lord, hath dashed in
die Fein - - des - macht, dein Arm hat, o Herr, zer - schlagen in
thy right hand, oh Lord, hath dashed in pie_ces, thy right hand, oh Lord, hath dashed in pieces the e_ne - my,
dein Arm hat, o Herr, zerschlagen in Stü_cke, dein Arm hat, o Herr, zerschlagen in Stücke die Fein_des - macht,
my, thy right hand, oh Lord, hath dashed in pie_ces, in pie_ces the e - ne - my,
macht, dein Arm hat, o Herr, zerschlagen in Stücke, in Stü_cke die Fein_des_ macht,
my, thy right hand, oh Lord, hath dashed in pie_ces the e - - - ne -
macht, dein Arm hat, o Herr, zerschlagen in Stücke die Fein - - des -
pieces
Stücke
the e - - ne - my, thy right hand, oh Lord, hath dashed in
die Fein - - des - macht, dein Arm hat, o Herr, zer - schlagen in
thy right hand, oh Lord, hath dashed in pie_ces, thy right hand, oh Lord, hath dashed in pieces, hath dashed in pie_ces the e_ne -
dein Arm hat, o Herr, zerschlagen in Stü_cke dein Arm hat, o Herr, zer_schlagen in Stücke, zer_schlagen in Stü_cke die Feindes -
my, thy right hand, oh Lord, hath dashed in pieces, hath dashed in pie_ces the e_ne -
macht, dein Arm hat, o Herr, zer_schlagen in Stü_cke, zer_schlagen in Stü_cke die Feindes -
my, thy right hand, oh Lord, hath dashed in pieces the e - - - ne -
macht, dein Arm hat, o Herr, zer_schlagen in Stü_cke die Fein - - - des -
Tasto solo.
Tutti.
fp
f

pie_ces, thy right hand, oh Lord,
Stü_cke,
thy right hand, oh Lord, hath dashed in pieces, hath dashed in pie_ces the e_ne_
dein Arm, o Herr,
dein Arm hat, o Herr, zer_schlagen in Stü_cke, zer_schlagen in Stü_cke die Fein_des_
thy right hand, oh Lord,
thy right hand, oh Lord, hath dashed in pieces, hath dashed in pie_ces the e_ne_
my, thy right hand, oh Lord,
macht, dein Arm, o Herr,
pie_ces, thy right hand, oh Lord,
Stü_cke,
my, dein Arm, o Herr,
macht,
my, thy right hand, oh Lord,
macht,
my, dein Arm, o Herr,
macht,
Soli. Tutti. Soli.
mp f mp

my,
macht,
my,
thy right hand, oh Lord, hath dash_ed in pie_ces, hath dash_ed in pie_ces the e_ne_my,
dein Arm hat, o Herr, zer_schlagen in Stü_cke, zer_schlagen in Stü_cke die Fein_desmacht,
thy right hand, oh
dein Arm, o
thy right hand, oh
dein Arm, o
thy right hand, oh Lord, hath dash_ed in pie_ces, hath dash_ed in pie_ces the e_ne_my, thy right hand, oh Lord,
dein Arm hat, o Herr, zer_schla_gen in Stü_cke, zerschlagen in Stü_cke die Fein_desmacht, dein Arm, o Herr,
thy right hand, oh Lord, hath dash_ed in pie_ces, hath dash_ed in pie_ces the e_ne_my, thy right hand, oh Lord,
dein Arm hat, o Herr, zer_schlagen in Stü_cke, zer_schlagen in Stü_cke die Fein_desmacht, dein Arm, o Herr,
Tutti.
Soli.

Lord, thy right hand, oh Lord, hath dash_ed in pie_ces, hath dash_ed in pie_ces the e_ne_my,
Herr, dein Arm hat, o Herr, zer_schla_gen in Stü_cke, zerschlagen in Stü_cke die Fein_des_macht,
Lord, thy right hand, oh Lord, hath dash_ed in pie_ces, hath dash_ed in pie_ces the e_ne_my,
Herr, dein Arm hat, o Herr, zer_schlagen in Stü_cke, zerschlagen in Stü_cke die Feindes_macht,
thy right hand, oh Lord, thy right hand, oh
dein Arm, o Herr, dein Arm hat, o
thy right hand, oh Lord, thy right hand, oh
dein Arm, o Herr, dein Arm hat, o

thy right hand, oh
Lord,
thy right hand, oh
dein Arm, o
Herr,
dein Arm hat, o
thy right hand, oh
Lord,
thy right hand, oh
dein Arm, o
Herr,
dein Arm hat, o
Lord, hath dash_ed in pie_ces, hath dash_ed in
pie_ces the e_ne_my, thy right hand, oh
Lord,
thy right hand, oh
Herr, zer_schlagen in Stü_cke, zer_schla_gen in
Stü_cke die Feindes_macht, dein Arm, o
Herr,
dein Arm hat, o
Lord, hath dash_ed in pie_ces, hath dash_ed in
pie_ces the e_ne_my, thy right hand, oh
Lord,
thy right hand, oh
Herr, zer_schlagen in Stü_cke, zer_schla_gen in
Stü_cke die Feindes_macht, dein Arm, o
Herr,
dein Arm hat, o
Tutti.
f
ff

Adagio.
Lord, hath dash_ed in pie_ces, hath dash_ed in pie_ces the e_ne_my. And in the great_ness of thine
Herr, zer_schlagen in Stü_cke, zer_schlagen in Stü_cke die Fein_des_macht. Und in der Grö_sse dei_ner
Lord, hath dash_ed in pie_ces, hath dash_ed in pie_ces the e_ne_my. And in the great_ness of thine
Herr, zer_schlagen in Stü_cke, zer_schlagen in Stü_cke die Fein_des_macht. Und in der Grö_sse dei_ner
Lord, hath dash_ed in pie_ces, hath dash_ed in pie_ces the e_ne_my. And in the great_ness of thine
Herr, zer_schlagen in Stü_cke, zer_schlagen in Stü_cke die Fein_des_macht. Und in der Grö_sse dei_ner
Lord, hath dash_ed in pie_ces, hath dash_ed in pie_ces the e_ne_my. And in the great_ness of thine
Herr, zer_schlagen in Stü_cke, zer_schlagen in Stü_cke die Fein_des_macht. Und in der Grö_sse dei_ner
tempo ad libitum.
Andante con moto.
f

ex - cel - len - cy, thou hast o - verthrown, thou hast o - verthrown them that rose up a - gainst thee.
Herr - lich - keit hast du sie ge - stürzt, hast du sie ge - stürzt all' die ge - gen dich strit - ten.
ex - cel - len - cy, thou hast o - verthrown, thou hast o - verthrown them that rose up a - gainst thee.
Herr - lich - keit hast du sie ge - stürzt, hast du sie ge - stürzt all' die ge - gen dich strit - ten.
ex - cel - len - cy, thou hast o - verthrown, thou hast o - verthrown them that rose up a - gainst thee.
Herr - lich - keit hast du sie ge - stürzt, hast du sie ge - stürzt all' die ge - gen dich strit - ten.
ex - cel - len - cy, thou hast o - verthrown, thou hast o - verthrown them that rose up a - gainst thee.
Herr - lich - keit hast du sie ge - stürzt, hast du sie ge - stürzt all' die ge - gen dich strit - ten.

CHORUS.

SOPRANO I.
Thou sent_est forth thy wrath, which con_-su_med them as stub_ble, thou sent_est forth thy
Du sand_test dei_nen Grimm, der ver_zehr_te sie wie Stop_peln, du sand_test dei_nen
ALTO I.
Thou sent_est forth thy
Du sand_test dei_nen
TENORE I.
BASSO I.
SOPRANO II.
ALTO II.
TENORE II.
BASSO II.
Tutti Bassi.
Organo.
wrath, thou sent_est forth thy wrath, thy wrath, thou
Grimm, du sand_test dei_nen Grimm, dei_nen Grimm, du
wrath, which con_sumed them as stub_ble, thou sent_est forth thy wrath,
Grimm, der ver_zehr_te sie wie Stop_peln, du sand_test dei_nen Grimm,
Thou sent_est forth thy wrath, which con_-su_med them as
Du sand_test dei_nen Grimm, der ver_zehr_te sie wie

sent - est forth thy wrath, which con - su - med them as stubble, thou sent - est
sand - test dei-nen Grimm, der ver- zehr - te sie wie Stoppeln, du sand - test
which con-su - med them as stubble, which con - su - med them, which con - su-med them as
der ver-zehr - te sie wie Stoppeln, der ver - zehr - te sie, der ver- zehr-te sie wie
stub-ble, thou sent - est forth thy wrath, thou sent - est
Stoppeln, du sand - test dei - nen Grimm, du sand - test
Thou sent - est forth thy wrath, which con - su-med them as stubble, thou sent - est
Du sand - test dei - nen Grimm, der ver - zehrte sie wie Stoppeln, du sand - test
forth thy wrath, thy wrath, thou sent - est forth thy wrath, thou sentest
dei - nen Grimm, dei-nen Grimm, du sand - test dei - nen Grimm, dei-nen
stub-ble, thou sent - est forth thy wrath, thou sent - est forth thy wrath, thou sentest
Stoppeln, thou sand - test dei - nen Grimm, du sand - test dei - nen Grimm, dei-nen
forth thy wrath, thou sent - est forth thy wrath, thou sentest
dei - nen Grimm, du sand - test dei - nen Grimm, dei-nen
forth thy wrath, thy wrath,
dei - nen Grimm, dei - nen Grimm,

Trombone I.
Trombone II.
Trombone III.
Oboe I.
Oboe II.
Fagotti.
Violino I.
Violino II.
Viola.
forth, thou sent-est forth thy wrath, thou sent - est
Grimm, du sand-test dei - nen Grimm, du sand - test
forth, thou sent - est forth thy wrath, thou
Grimm, du sand - test dei - nen Grimm, du
forth, thou sent-est forth thy wrath, thou sent - est, thou sent - est
Grimm, du sand-test dei - nen Grimm, du sand - test, du sand - test
thou sent - est forth thy wrath, which con - su-med them as stub-ble, thou
du sand - test dei - nen Grimm, der ver - zehr-te sie wie Stop-peln, du
Thou, thou sent-est forth thy wrath, which con - su-med them as stub-ble,
Du, du sand - test dei - nen Grimm, der ver - zehr-te sie wie Stop-peln,
Thou sent - est forth thy wrath, which con - su-med them as stub-ble,
Du sand - test dei - nen Grimm, der ver - zehr-te sie wie Stop-peln,
Tutti.

forth, thou sent - est forth thy wrath, thy wrath, thou
dei - nen, sand - test dei - nen Grimm, dei_nen Grimm, du
sent - est forth, thou sent - est forth thy wrath,
sand - test dei - nen, sand - test dei - - - - - nen Grimm,
forth, thou sent - est forth, thou sent - est forth thy wrath, thou
dei - nen Grimm, du sand - test, sand - test dei - - - nen Grimm, du
sent - est forth, thou sent - est forth thy wrath, thou sent_est
sand - test dei - nen, sand - test dei - - nen Grimm, du sandtest
as stub_ble, as stubble, as stub_ble, which con_ sumed, which con_ sumed them as stubble,
wie Stoppeln, wie Stoppeln, wie Stoppeln, der ver_ zehr_te, der ver_ zehr_te sie wie Stoppeln,
as stub_ble, as stub_ble, as stub_ble, which con_ sumed, con_ sumed them as stubble,
wie Stoppeln, wie Stoppeln, wie Stoppeln, der ver_ zehr_te, der ver_ zehr_te sie wie Stoppeln,
mp

sent _ est forth thy wrath, thou sent _ est forth
sand _ test dei _ nen Grimm, du sandtest dei _
thou sent _ est forth; thou sent _ est forth thy wrath, thou sent _ est
du sand _ test dei _ nen, sandtest dei _ nen Grimm, du sand _ test
sent _ est forth, thou sent _ est
sandtest dei _ nen Grimm, du sand _ test
forth thy wrath, thou sent _ est
dei _ nen Grimm, du sand _ test
thou sent _ est
du sand _ test
thou sent _ est
du sand _ test
thou sent _ est
du sand _ test
thou sent _ est
du sand _ test

thy wrath, thou sentest forth thy wrath, which con - sumed them, thou
- nen Grimm, du sandtest dei - nen Grimm, der ver - zehr-te sie, du
forth thy wrath, thou sent - est forth thy wrath, which con - su-med them as stubble,
dei - nen Grimm, du sand - test dei-nen Grimm, der ver- zehr-te sie wie Stoppeln,
forth thy wrath, thou sent - est forth, thou sent - est forth,
dei - nen Grimm, du sand - test, sand - test dei - nen Grimm,
forth thy wrath, which con - su - med them as stubble, thou sent - est forth, thou
dei - nen Grimm, der ver - zehr - te sie wie Stoppeln, du sand - test, du
forth thy wrath, which con - su - med them as stubble, thou
dei - nen Grimm, der ver - zehr - te sie wie Stoppeln, du
forth thy wrath, thy wrath, which con - sumed them as stubble, thou
dei-nen Grimm, den Grimm, der ver-zehr-te sie wie Stoppeln, du
forth thy wrath, which con - su - med them as stubble, thou
dei - nen Grimm, der ver - zehr - te sie wie Stoppeln, du
forth thy wrath, which con - su - med them as stubble, thou
dei - nen Grimm, der ver - zehr - te sie wie Stoppeln, du

sent _ est forth, thou sent _ est forth thy wrath,
sand _ test dei _ nen, sand _ test dei - nen Grimm,
thou sent - est forth, thou sent _ est
du sand - test dei - nen Grimm, sand _ test
thou sent - est forth thy wrath, which con_ su_med, which con_
du sand - test dei - nen Grimm, der ver_ zehr_te, der ver_
sent _ est forth, thou sent _ est forth thy wrath, which con_ su_med, which con_
sand _ test dei _ nen, sand _ test dei - nen Grimm, der ver_ zehr_te, der ver_
sent _ est forth, thou sent _ est forth thy wrath, which con_
sand _ test dei _ nen, sand _ test dei - nen Grimm, der ver_
sent _ est forth, thou sent _ est forth thy wrath, which con_
sand _ test dei _ nen, sand _ test dei - nen Grimm, der ver_
sent _ est forth, thou sent _ est forth thy wrath, thy wrath, which con_ su_med, which con_
sand _ test, du sand _ test dei _ nen Grimm, dei_nen Grimm, der ver_ zehr_te, der ver_
sent _ est forth, thou sent _ est forth thy wrath, which con_ su_med, which con_
sand _ test dei _ nen, sand _ test dei - nen Grimm, der ver_ zehr_te, der ver_

thou sent - - - est forth thy wrath, which con -
du sand - - - test dei - nen Grimm, der ver -
forth thy wrath, thou sent - est forth thy wrath, which con -
dei - - - nen Grimm, du sand - test dei - nen Grimm, der ver -
su - med them, thou sent - est forth thy wrath, which con -
zehr - te sie, du sand - test dei - - nen Grimm, der ver -
su - med them as stub - ble, thou sent - est forth thy wrath, which con - su - med, which con -
zehr - te sie wie Stoppeln, du sand - test dei - nen Grimm, der ver - zehr - te, der ver -
su - med them as stub - ble, which con - su - med them, which con - su - - -
zehr - te sie wie Stoppeln, der ver - zehr - te sie, der ver - zehr - - -
su - med them as stub - ble, which con - su - med them, which con - su - med
zehr - te sie wie Stoppeln, der ver - zehr - te sie, der ver - zehr - te
su - med them as stub - ble, which con - su - med them, which con - su - med, which con -
zehr - te sie wie Stoppeln, der ver - zehr - te sie, der ver - zehr - te, der ver -
su - med them as stub - ble, which con - su - med them, which con - su - - - -
zehr - te sie wie Stoppeln, der ver - zehr - te sie, der ver - zehr - - - -
4 3 7 6 ♯ 6

su - med them as stub - ble, which con - su - - - med, which con -
zehr - te sie wie Stoppeln, der ver - zehr - - - te, der ver -
su-med them as stub-ble, which con - su - med them, which con -
zehr-te sie wie Stoppeln, der ver - zehr - te sie, der ver -
su - med them as stub-ble, which con - su - med, which con -
zehr - te sie wie Stoppeln, der ver - zehr - te, der ver -
su - med them as stub-ble, which con - su - med them, which con -
zehr - te sie wie Stoppeln, der ver - zehr - te sie, der ver -
- med them as stub-ble, which con - su - med
- te sie wie Stoppeln, der ver - zehr - te
them, which con-su-med them as stub-ble, which con - su-med them, which con -
sie, der ver-zehr-te sie wie Stoppeln, der ver - zehr-te sie, der ver -
su - med them as stub-ble, which con-su-med them as stub-ble, which con -
zehr - te sie wie Stoppeln, der ver-zehr-te sie wie Stop-peln, der ver -
- med them as stub-ble, which con - su - med them, which con -
- te sie wie Stoppeln, der ver - zehr - te sie, der ver -

su_med them as stub_ble, as stub_ble, which con_su_med them as stub_ble.
zehr_te sie wie Stoppeln, wie Stoppeln, der ver_zehr_te sie wie Stoppeln.
su_med them as stub_ble, as stub_ble, which con_su_med them as stub_ble.
zehr_te sie wie Stoppeln, wie Stoppeln, der ver_zehr_te sie wie Stoppeln.
them as stub_ble, as stub_ble, which con_su_med them as stub_ble.
sie wie Stoppeln, wie Stoppeln, der ver_zehr_te sie wie Stoppeln.
su_med them as stub_ble, as stub_ble, which con_su_med them as stub_ble.
zehr_te sie wie Stoppeln, wie Stoppeln, der ver_zehr_te sie wie Stoppeln.

CHORUS.

Oboe I. II.
Violino I.
mezzo piano
piano
Violino II.
Viola.
SOPRANO.
And with the
Und vor dem
ALTO.
And with the blast of thy
Und vor dem Hauch dei - nes
TENORE.
And with the blast of thy nostrils
Und vor dem Hauch dei - nes Mundes
BASSO.
And with the blast
Und vor dem Hauch
Bassi.
Andante con moto.
p
Pianoforte.
blast of thy nos - trils the wa - ters were ga - ther - ed, were
Hauch dei - nes Mun - des zer - theil - ten sich al - so - bald, sich
nos - trils the wa - ters were ga - ther - ed to - ge - ther, the wa - ters were
Mun - des zer - theil - ten sich al - so - bald die Was - ser, zer - theil - ten sich
the wa - ters were ga - ther - ed to - ge - ther,
zer - theil - ten sich al - so - bald die Was - ser,
of thy nos - trils the wa - ters were ga - ther - ed to - ge - ther,
dei - nes Mun - des zer - theil - ten sich al - so - bald die Was - ser,

ga - - - ther_ed to - ge - ther, and with the blast of thy
al - - - so_bald die Was - ser, und vor dem Hauch dei - nes
ga - - - ther_ed to - ge - ther, and with the blast
al - - - so_bald die Was - ser, und vor dem Hauch
were ga_ther_ed to - ge - ther, and with the
zer_ theil_ten sich die Was - ser, und vor dem
were ga_ther_ed to - ge - ther,
zer_ theil_ten sich die Was - ser,
mf
nos_trils the wa - ters were ga - ther_ed to_ge_ther,
Mun_des zer_theil - ten sich al - so_bald die Was_ser,
of thy nos_trils the wa - ters were ga_ther_ed to - ge_ther, were
dei_nes Mun_des zer_ -theil - ten sich al - so_bald die Was_ser, zer_
blast of thy nos_trils the wa - ters were
Hauch dei - nes Mun_des zer_theil - ten sich
and with the blast of thy nos_trils the wa - ters were ga - ther_ed, were
und vor dem Hauch dei - nes Mun_des zer_ -theil - ten sich al - so_bald, sich
5 6 4 3

Oboe I.
Oboe II.
the floods stood up - right, stood up right as an heap,
die Flut stand auf - recht, stand auf - recht wie ein Wall,
ga - ther - ed to - ge - ther,
theil - ten sich die Was - ser,
the floods stood
die Flut stand
ga - ther - ed to - ge - ther,
al - so - bald die Was - ser,
the floods stood
die Flut stand
ga - ther - ed to - ge - ther,
al - so - bald die Was - ser,
mp
fp
up - - right as an heap, the floods stood up - right, stood up - right as an
auf - - recht wie ein Wall, die Flut stand auf - recht, stand auf - recht wie ein
up - - right as an heap,
auf - - recht wie ein Wall,
mp

Oboe I.
Oboe II.
forte
forte
the floods stood up - right as an heap,
die Flut stand auf - recht wie ein Wall,
heap,
Wall,
the floods stood up - right as an heap,
die Flut stand auf - recht wie ein Wall,
and the
und die
forte
fp
f
piano
depths were con - geal - ed in the heart of the
Tie - fe er - star - re - te im Her - zen der
piano
p

unis.
piano
forte
the floods stood up - right as an heap,
die Flut stand auf - recht wie ein Wall,
the wa - ters were ga - ther - ed to - ge - ther, the wa - ters were
zer - theil - ten sich al - so - bald die Was - ser, zer - theil - ten sich
the wa - ters were ga - ther - ed to - ge - ther, the
zer - theil - ten sich al - so - bald die Was - ser, die
sea,
See,
as an heap, as an heap,
wie ein Wall, wie ein Wall,
ga - ther - ed, the wa - ters were ga - thered, the wa - ters were ga - ther - ed to - ge - ther, the
al - so - bald, zer - theil - ten sich al - sobald, zer - theil - ten sich al - sobald die Was - ser, zer -
depths were con - geal - ed, the depths were con - geal - ed, the depths were con - geal - ed,
Tie - fe er - starr - te, die Tie - fe er - starr - te, die Tie - fe er - starr - te,
cresc.

as an heap, as an
wie ein Wall, wie ein
wa _ ters were ga _ ther_ed to _ ge _ ther, were ga _ ther_ed to _ ge _ ther, were ga _ ther_ed to _
theil _ ten sich al _ so_bald die Was _ ser, zer _ theil _ ten sich die Was _ ser, zer _ theil _ ten sich die
the depths were con _ geal _ ed in the heart
die Tie _ fe er _ starr _ te in dem Her _
in the heart
in dem Her _
heap, as an heap, the depths were con _
Wall, wie ein Wall, die Tie _ fe er _
ge _ ther, were ga _ ther_ed to _ ge _ ther,
Was _ ser, zer _ theil _ ten sich die Was _ ser,
of the sea, the depths were con _ geal _ ed, were con _
zen der See, die Tie _ fe er _ star _ re _ te, er _
of the sea, the depths
zen der See, die Tie _

geal_ed, were con_ geal_ed in the heart of the sea,
star_re_te, er_ _star_re_te im Her_zen der See,
the depths were con_ geal_ed in the heart of the sea, the floods stood up_right as an
die Tie_fe er_ _star_re_te im Her_zen der See, die Flut stand auf_recht wie ein
geal _ ed in the heart of the sea,
star _ re_te im Her_zen der See,
were con_ geal_ed in the heart of the sea,
fe er_ _star_re_te im Her_zen der See,
the wa_ters were ga_ther_ed to_
zer_ _theil_ten sich al_so_bald die
heap,
Wall,
the wa_ters were ga_ther_ed to_ _ge_ther, were ga_ther_ed to_
zer_ _theil_ten sich al_so_bald die Was_ser, zer_theil_ten sich die
the wa_ters were ga_ther_ed to_ge_ther, were ga_ther_ed to_
zer_theil_ten sich al_so_bald die Was_ser, zer_theil_ten sich die

ge - - - ther, the floods stood up - right as an heap,
Was - - - ser, die Flut stand auf - recht wie ein Wall,
the wa - ters were ga - ther-ed to - ge - ther, the
zer - theil - ten sich al - so-bald die Was - ser, zer -
ge - - - ther, the depths were con - geal - - ed,
Was - - - ser, die Tie - fe er - starr - te,
ge - - ther
Was - - ser
6
6
as an heap, as an
wie ein Wall, wie ein
wa - ters were ga - ther-ed to - ge - ther, the wa - ters were ga - ther-ed to -
theil - ten sich al - so-bald die Was - ser, zer - theil - ten sich al - so-bald die
the depths were con - geal - - ed, the
die Tie - fe er - starr - te, die
6
6

heap,
Wall,
ge - ther,
Was - ser
depths were con - geal - - ed
Tie - - fe er - starr - - te
in the heart of the
in dem Her - - - zen der
piano
p
forte
(mp)
the depths were con - geal - ed, were con - - geal - - ed
die Tie - fe er - star - re - te, er - - star - - re -
the depths were con - geal - ed, con - - geal - ed, were con - - geal - - ed
die Tie - - fe er - starr - te, er - - star - re - te, er - - star - - re -
sea, were con - geal - - - ed, con - - geal - - ed
See, er - - starr - - - te, er - - star - - re -
sea, the depths were con - geal - - ed
See, die Tie - fe er - star - - re -
mf
mp

Oboe I.
Oboe II.
unis.
forte
in the heart of the sea.
te im Her_ zen der See.
in the heart of the sea.
te im Her_ zen der See.
in the heart of the sea.
te im Her_ zen der See.
in the heart of the sea.
te im Her_ zen der See.
4 3
6 6
Violonc.
Tutti.
tempo ad libit.
a tempo.
f

Andante.
Violino I.
Violino II.
Viola.
TENORE.
Tutti Bassi.
Andante.
Pianoforte.
f
The e-ne-my said:
So sag-te der Feind:
I will pur-sue,
ich ei-le nach,
I will o-ver-take,
bis ich sie er-hascht,
mp

I will o-ver take,
bis ich sie er hascht,
I will pur-sue, I'll o-ver take, I will di
ich ei-le nach, bis ich er-hascht, bis ich ge-
vide,
thei
I'll di vide,
let den Raub,
I will pur sue,
ich ei-le nach,
I will o-ver take,
bis ich sie er hascht,
I will di vide the spoil;
bis ich ge theilt den Raub;

the e-ne-my said: I will pur-
so sag-te der Feind: ich ei-le
sue, I will o-ver-take, I will pur-sue, I'll o-ver-take, I will di-
nach, bis ich sie er-hascht, ich ei-le nach, bis ich er-hascht, bis ich ge-
vide the spoil: my lust shall be sa-tis-fied
theilt den Raub, und stil-le die Ra-che-lust

up - on them: I will draw my sword: my hand shall de - stroy
an ih - nen; ich will ziehn mein Schwert, mein Arm soll sie ver - der
piano
stroy them, I will draw my sword: my hand shall de - stroy
der ben, ich will ziehn mein Schwert, mein Arm soll sie ver - der
them, my hand shall de - stroy them. I will pur-
ben, mein Arm soll sie ver - der - ben. Ich ei - le

sue, I'll o-ver-take, I will di-vide, I'll draw my sword: my hand shall de-stroy
nach, bis ich er-hascht, bis ich ge-theilt, ich zieh' mein Schwert: mein Arm soll sie ver-der
them, my hand, my hand shall de-stroy them.
ben, mein Arm, mein Arm soll sie ver-der-ben.
ritard.
a tempo.
ritard.

Andante larghetto.
Oboe I.
Oboe II.
SOPRANO.
Organo, Violoncelli, Fagotti, e Viola.
Viola 8va alta.
Contrabassi.
Andante larghetto.
Pianoforte.
mf
p
Thou didst blow, thou didst blow with the wind, thou didst blow with the
Aber Du liessest weh'n deinen Hauch, liessest weh'n deinen

wind: the sea co - ver'd them, they sank as
Hauch: das Meer deck - te sie, sie san_ken wie
lead, they sank as lead, as lead in the mighty wa - - -
Blei, sie san - ken wie Blei, wie Blei in dem mächt'gen Was - - -
ters, they sank as lead, as
ser, sie san_ken wie Blei, wie

lead in the mighty wa - - - - - - - ters, they sank, they sank as
Blei in dem mächt'gen Was - - - - - - - ser, sie san_ken, sie san_ken wie
lead in the migh_ty wa - - - - - - - ters, in the mighty wa_ters; thou didst
Blei in dem mächt'gen Was - - - - - - ser, in dem mächt'gen Was_ser; a_ber
blow, thou didst blow with the wind: the sea co_ver'd them, they sank, they sank as
Du lie_ssest weh'n dei_nen Hauch: das Meer deck_te sie, sie san_ken wie das

lead, they sank as lead in the migh_ty wa
Blei, sie san_ken wie Blei in dem mächt'gen Was
ters, as lead in the migh_ty wa ters.
ser, wie Blei in dem mächt'gen Was ser.
Tutti.
mf

CHORUS.

Grave.
Oboe I.
Oboe II.
Fagotto I.
Fagotto II.
Violino I.
Violino II.
Viola.
SOPRANO I.
Who is like un - to Thee, oh Lord, a - mong the Gods?
ALTO I.
Wer ver - glei - chet sich Dir, o Herr, un - ter den Göt - tern?
TENORE I.
Who is like un - to Thee, oh Lord, a - mong the Gods?
BASSO I.
Wer ver - glei - chet sich Dir, o Herr, un - ter den Göt - tern?
SOPRANO II.
Who is like un - to Thee, oh Lord, a - mong the Gods?
ALTO II.
Wer ver - glei - chet sich Dir, o Herr, un - ter den Göt - tern?
TENORE II.
Who is like un - to Thee, oh Lord, a - mong the Gods?
BASSO II.
Wer ver - glei - chet sich Dir, o Herr, un - ter den Göt - tern?
Tutti Bassi, e Organo.
Grave, ma non adagio.
Pianoforte.

who is like Thee, glo - rious in ho - li - ness, fear - ful in prai - ses, do - ing
wer glei - chet Dir, glanz - voll in Hei - lig - keit, schreck - lich und herr - lich, wun - der -
who is like Thee, glo - rious in ho - li - ness, fear - ful in prai - ses, do - ing
wer glei - chet Dir, glanz - voll in Hei - lig - keit, schreck - lich und herr - lich, wun - der -
who is like Thee, glo - rious in ho - li - ness, fear - ful in prai - ses, do - ing
wer glei - chet Dir, glanz - voll in Hei - lig - keit, schreck - lich und herr - lich, wun - der -
who is like Thee, glo - rious in ho - li - ness, fear - ful in prai - ses, do - ing
wer glei - chet Dir, glanz - voll in Hei - lig - keit, schreck - lich und herr - lich, wun - der -

won_ders, fear_ful in prai_ses, do_ing won_ders! Thou stret_chest out thy right hand:
thä_tig, schrecklich und herr_lich, wun_der_ thä_tig! Du streck_test aus die Rech_te:
won_ders, fear_ful in prai_ses, do_ing won_ders! Thou stret_chest out thy right hand:
thä_tig, schrecklich und herr_lich, wun_der_ thä_tig! Du streck_test aus die Rech_te:
won_ders, fear_ful in prai_ses, do_ing won_ders! Thou stret_chest out thy right hand:
thä_tig, schrecklich und herr_lich, wun_der_ thä_tig! Du streck_test aus die Rech_te:
won_ders, fear_ful in prai_ses, do_ing won_ders! Thou stret_chest out thy right hand:
thä_tig, schrecklich und herr_lich, wun_der_ thä_tig! Du streck_test aus die Rech_te:
più f

Trombone I.
Trombone II.
Trombone III.
Oboe I.
Oboe II.
Fagotti.
Violino I.
Violino II.
Viola.
SOPRANO I.
The earth swal - - low'd them,
Da ver - schlang sie das Grab,
ALTO I.
TENORE I.
The earth swal - - - low'd them, the earth
Da ver - schlang sie das Grab, da ver -
BASSO I.
The earth swal - - - low'd them, the earth swal - low'd, swal - - - - -
Da ver - schlang sie das Grab, da ver - schlang, ver - schlang
SOPRANO II.
ALTO II.
TENORE II.
BASSO II.
The earth swal - - - low'd them,
Da ver - schlang sie das Grab,
Bassi, e Cembalo.
Organo.
tasto solo.
Alla breve.
mf

the earth swal - - low'd them, the earth
da ver - schlang sie das Grab, da ver -
The earth swal - - low'd them, the earth swal - - low'd, swal-low'd
Da ver - schlang sie das Grab, da ver - schlang, ver - schlang sie das
swal-low'd, swal - low'd them, the earth swal-low'd
schlang, ver - schlang sie das Grab, da ver - schlang, ver -
low'd them, the earth swal-low'd, swal-low'd
sie das Grab, da ver - schlang, ver - schlang sie das
The earth swal - low'd them, the earth
Da ver - schlang sie das Grab, da ver -
The earth swal - low'd them,
Da ver - schlang sie das Grab,
The earth swal-low'd,
Da ver - schlang, ver -
the earth swal-low'd, swallow'd
da ver - schlang, ver - schlang sie das

swal - low'd them, swal - low'd them, the earth swallow'd them, swal -
schlang sie das Grab, ver - schlang, verschlang, da verschlang sie, ver - schlang,
them, the earth swal - low'd them, the earth swal - low'd them, the earth
Grab, da ver - schlang sie das Grab, da ver-schlang sie das Grab, da ver-
swal - low'd them, the earth swal - low'd them,
schlang sie das Grab, da ver-schlang sie das Grab, ver-
them, the earth swal - low'd them, the earth swallow'd, swal - low'd them, the
Grab, da ver - schlang sie das Grab, da ver-schlang, ver - schlang sie das Grab, da
swallow'd, the earth swallow'd them, the earth swal - low'd, the
schlang sie, da ver-schlang sie das Grab, da ver-schlang sie, ver-
the earth swallow'd, swal - low'd them, the earth swal - low'd them,
da ver-schlang, ver - schlang sie das Grab, da ver-schlang sie das Grab,
swal - low'd them, the earth swal - low'd them, swallow'd,
schlang sie das Grab, verschlang sie das Grab, schlang sie,
them, the earth swal - low'd them, the earth swallow'd, swal - low'd them, the
Grab, da ver - schlang sie das Grab, da verschlang, ver - schlang sie das Grab, da

low'd, swal - low'd them.
ver - schlang sie das Grab.
swal - low'd them.
schlang sie das Grab.
swal - low'd them.
schlang sie das Grab.
earth swal - low'd them.
ver - schlang sie das Grab.
earth swal - low'd them, the earth swal - low'd them.
schlang, da ver - schlang sie das Grab.
swal - low'd, swal - low'd, swal - low'd, swal - low'd them.
schlang sie, schlang sie, da ver - schlang sie das Grab.
swal - low'd, swal - low'd, swal - low'd, the earth swal - low'd them.
schlang sie, schlang sie, schlang sie, da ver - schlang sie das Grab.
earth swal - low'd them.
ver - schlang sie das Grab.

Larghetto.
Violino I.
Violino II.
ALTO.
TENORE.
Bassi.
Larghetto.
Pianoforte.
mf
tr
Thou in thy mer - - cy hast led forth thy
Du in dei_ner Gna - - - de hast dein Volk ge_
mp
peo_ple which thou hast re_deem ed, which thou hast re_deem_ed,
lei_tet, das du hast er_lö_set, das du hast er_lö_set,
Thou in thy
Du in deiner
p

mer - - - cy hast led forth thy peo_ple which thou hast ___ re_deem - ed, which thou hast ___
Gna - - - de hast dein Volk ge - lei_tet, das du hast ___ er - lö - set, das du hast ___
thou in thy mer - - - cy hast led forth thy peo - ple which thou
du in dei_ner Gna - - - de hast dein Volk ge - lei - tet, das du
re - deem - ed, thou in thy mer - - - cy hast led forth thy
er - lö - set, du in dei_ner Gna - - - de hast dein Volk ge - -
hast ___ re - deem - - - ed, thy peo - ple which thou hast re - deem - -
hast ___ er - lö - - - - set, dein Volk, das du hast er - lö - -
peo - ple which thou hast ___ re - deem - ed, which thou hast re - deem - - - -
lei - tet, das du hast ___ er - lö - set, das du hast er - lö - - - -

ed, which thou hast re-deem
set, das du hast er-lö
ed, thy peo-ple which thou hast re-deem
set, dein Volk, das du hast er-lö
ed.
set.
ed.
set.
Thou hast guided them in thy
Und du hast geführt sie mit
Thou hast guided them in thy strength, thou hast guided them in thy strength
Und du hast ge-führt sie mit Macht, und du hast ge-führt sie mit Macht
strength, in thy strength, in thy strength un-
Macht, mit Macht, mit Macht zu

un- to thy holy habi- ta- tion,
zu deiner heiligen Woh- nung,
to thy holy habi- ta- tion,
deiner heiligen Woh- nung,
tr
p
mf
thou hast guided them in thy strength
und du hast geführt sie mit Macht
thou hast guided them in thy strength unto thy holy habi-
und du hast geführt sie mit Macht zu deiner heiligen

ta - tion,
Woh - nung,
thou hast guided them in thy strength
und du hast ge-führt sie mit Macht
un - to thy ho - ly ha - bi - ta - tion,
zu dei - ner hei - li-gen Wohnung,
thou hast guided them in thy strength
und du hast ge-führt sie mit Macht
un - to thy ho - ly ha - bi - tation.
zu dei - ner hei - li - gen Woh - nung.
un - to thy ho - ly ha - bi - ta - tion.
zu dei - ner hei - li - gen Woh - nung.

CHORUS.

Largo, e staccato.
Oboe I.
Oboe II.
Fagotti.
Violino I.
Violino II.
Viola.
SOPRANO I.
ALTO I.
TENORE I.
BASSO I.
SOPRANO II.
ALTO II.
TENORE II.
BASSO II.
Bassi, e Cembalo.
Organo.
Largo, non adagio, e staccato.
Pianoforte
mf

The peo - ple shall hear,
Das hö - ren die Völ - ker,
the peo - ple shall hear,
das hö - ren die Völ - ker,
shall
die
6
6 4
5 ♯
6
6
cresc.

the people shall hear, and be a - fraid, and be a - fraid, and be a -
das hö - ren die Völ - ker und sind er - staunt, und sind er - staunt, und sind er -
hear, shall hear, and be a - fraid, and be a - fraid, and be a -
Völ - - ker, die Völ - ker und sind er - staunt, und sind er - staunt, und sind er -
the peo - ple shall hear, and be a - fraid, and be a - fraid, and be a -
das hö - ren die Völ - ker und sind er - staunt, und sind er - staunt, und sind er -
hear, and be a - fraid, and be a - fraid, and be a -
Völ - - - - - - ker und sind er - staunt, und sind er - staunt, und sind er -
the peo - ple shall hear, and be a - fraid, and be a - fraid, and be a -
das hö - ren die Völ - ker und sind er - staunt, und sind er - staunt, und sind er -
hear, shall hear, and be a - fraid, and be a - fraid, and be a -
Völ - - ker, die Völ - ker und sind er - staunt, und sind er - staunt, und sind er -
hear, shall hear, and be a - fraid, and be a - fraid, and be a -
Völ - - ker, die Völ - ker und sind er - staunt, und sind er - staunt, und sind er -
hear, shall hear, and be a - fraid, and be a - fraid, and be a -
Völ - - ker, die Völ - ker und sind er - staunt, und sind er - staunt, und sind er -

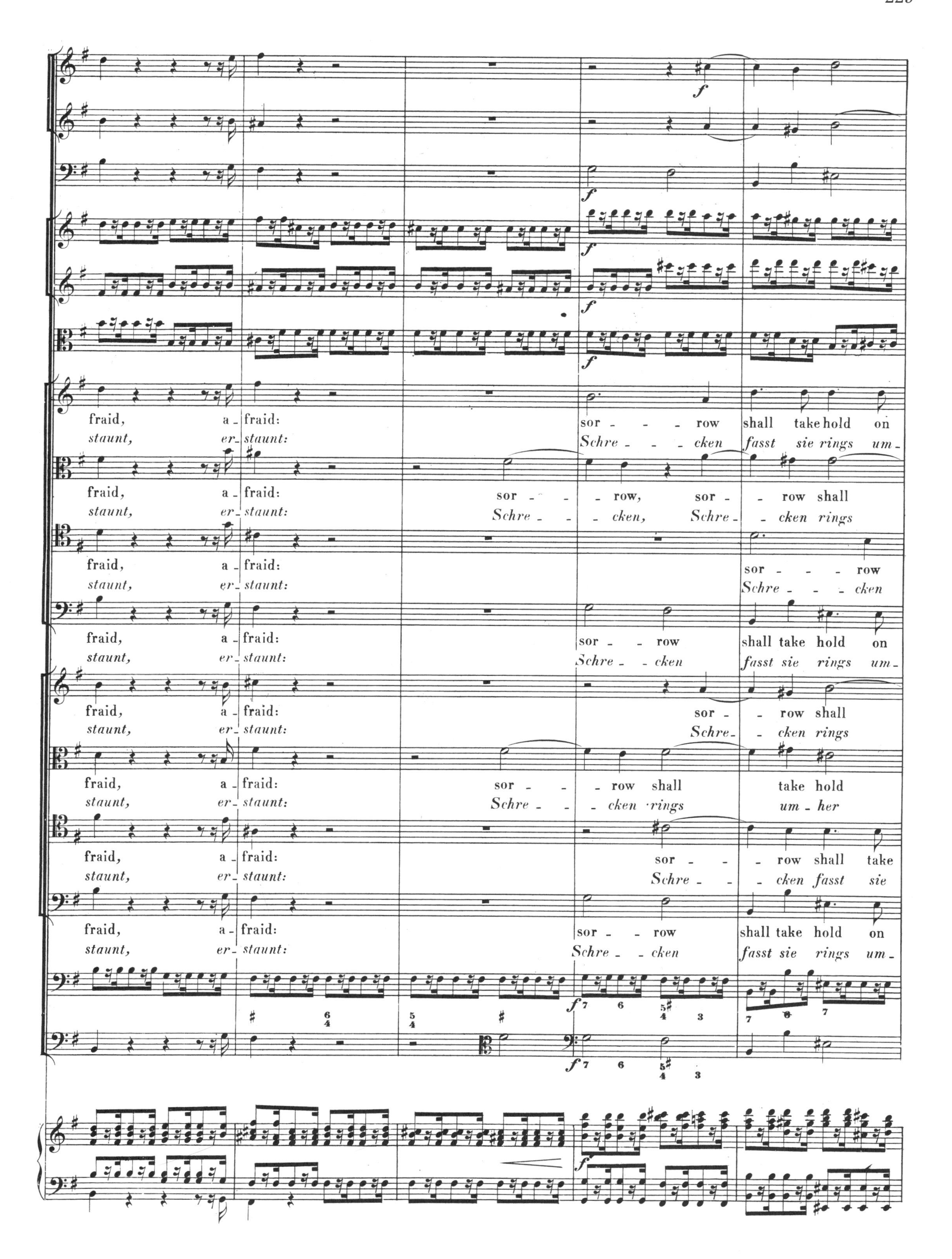
fraid, a - fraid: sor - - - row shall take hold on
staunt, er - staunt: Schre - - - cken fasst sie rings um -
fraid, a - fraid: sor - - row, sor - - row shall
staunt, er - staunt: Schre - - cken, Schre - - cken rings
fraid, a - fraid: sor - - - row
staunt, er - staunt: Schre - - - cken
fraid, a - fraid: sor - - row shall take hold on
staunt, er - staunt: Schre - - cken fasst sie rings um -
fraid, a - fraid: sor - - row shall
staunt, er - staunt: Schre - - cken rings
fraid, a - fraid: sor - - - row shall take hold
staunt, er - staunt: Schre - - - cken rings um - her
fraid, a - fraid: sor - - - row shall take
staunt, er - staunt: Schre - - - cken fasst sie
fraid, a - fraid: sor - - row shall take hold on
staunt, er - staunt: Schre - - cken fasst sie rings um -

them, shall take hold on them, shall take hold on them;
her, rings um-her, um-her, fasst sie rings um-her;
take hold, shall take hold, shall take hold on them;
um-her, rings um-her, fasst sie rings um-her;
shall take hold on them, shall take hold on them;
fasst sie rings um-her, fasst sie rings um-her;
them, shall take hold, shall take hold, shall take hold on them;
her, rings um-her, rings um-her, fasst sie rings um-her;
take hold, shall take hold, shall take hold on them;
um-her, rings um-her, fasst sie rings um-her;
shall take hold, shall take hold on them;
rings um-her, fasst sie rings um-her;
hold on them, shall take hold on them;
rings um-her, fasst sie rings um-her;
them, shall take hold, shall take hold on them, shall take hold on them;
her, rings um-her, fasst sie rings um-her, fasst sie rings um-her;

all th'in-ha-bitants of Ca-naan shall melt a-way, all th'in-ha - bi-tants of
all die Ein-gebornen Ka-naan's er-greift die Angst, all die Ein - ge-bor-nen
all th'in-ha-bitants of Ca-naan shall melt a-way, shall
all die Ein-gebornen Ka-naan's er - greift die Angst, er -
all th'in-ha-bitants of Ca-naan shall melt a-way, shall melt, shall
all die Ein-gebornen Ka-naan's er - greift die Angst, er - greift, er -
all th'in-ha-bitants of Ca-naan shall melt a-way, shall
all die Ein-gebornen Ka-naan's er - greift die Angst, er -
all th'in-ha-bitants of Ca-naan shall melt a-way, all th'in-ha - bi-tants of
all die Ein-gebornen Ka-naan's er - greift die Angst, all die Ein - ge-bor-nen
all th'in-ha-bitants of Ca-naan shall
all die Ein-gebornen Ka-naan's er -
all th'in-ha-bitants of Ca-naan shall melt a - way, shall melt, shall
all die Ein-gebornen Ka-naan's er-greift die Angst, er - greift, er -
all th'in-ha-bitants of Ca-naan shall
all die Ein-gebornen Ka-naan's er -

Ca - na - an,
Ka - na - an's,
all th'in-ha-bitants of
all die Ein-ge-bornen
Ca - naan
Ka - naan's
shall
er -
melt a - way,
greift die Angst,
melt a - way, all th'in-
greift die Angst, all die
cresc.

melt a - way, shall melt a - way, all th'in - ha - bi - tants of Ca - na - an shall melt a - way,
greift die Angst, er - greift die Angst, all die Einge - bornen Ka - na - an's er - greift die Angst,
ha - bi - tants of Ca - - - - - - na - an shall melt a - way, shall melt a - way,
Einge - bornen Ka - - - - - - na - an's er - greift die Angst, er - greift die Angst,
shall melt a - way, all th'in - ha - bi - tants of Ca - na - an shall melt a - way,
er - greift die Angst, all die Einge - bornen Ka - na - an's er - greift die Angst,
shall
er -
shall
er -

shall melt a - way, shall
er - greift die Angst, er -
shall melt a - way, shall melt a - way, shall
er - greift die Angst, er - greift die Angst, er -
shall melt a - way, all th'in - ha - bitants of Ca - - -
er - greift die Angst, all die Einge - bornen Ka - - -
melt a - way, all th'in - ha - bitants of Ca - naan shall melt a - way, shall melt a - way, shall
greift die Angst, all die Einge - bornen Ka - naan's er - greift die Angst, er - greift die Angst, er -
shall melt a - way, all th'in - ha - bi - tants of Ca - naan shall
er - greift die Angst, all die Einge - bornen Ka - naan's er -
melt a - way, all th'in - ha - bi - tants of Ca - naan shall melt a - way,
greift die Angst, all die Einge - bornen Ka - naan's er - greift die Angst,
shall melt a - way, all th'in - ha - bi - tants of Ca - - -
er - greift die Angst, all die Einge - bornen Ka - - -
cresc.

melt a-way, shall melt a-way, all th'in - ha - bitants of Ca-na-an shall melt, shall
greift die Angst, er - greift die Angst, all die Ein-gebornen Ka-naan's er - greift, er -
melt a-way, shall melt a-way, all th'in - ha - bitants of Ca-na-an shall melt a-way,
greift die Angst, er - greift die Angst, all die Ein-gebornen Ka-naan's er - greift die Angst,
all th'in-ha - bi - tants of Ca-na-an shall melt, shall
all die Ein - ge - bor - nen Ka-naan's er - greift, er -
na-an shall melt a-way, shall melt
na-an's er - greift die Angst, er - greift
melt a-way, shall melt a-way, all th'in - ha - bitants of Ca-na-an shall melt, shall
greift die Angst, er - greift die Angst, all die Ein-gebornen Ka-naan's er - greift, er -
melt a-way, shall melt a-way, all th'in - ha - bitants of Ca-na-an shall melt a-way,
greift die Angst, er - greift die Angst, all die Ein-gebornen Ka-naan's er - greift die Angst,
all th'in-ha - bi - tants of Ca-na-an shall melt, shall
all die Ein - ge - bor - nen Ka-naan's er - greift, er -
na-an shall melt a-way, shall melt
na-an's er - greift die Angst, er - greift
sf
cresc.

melt a - way, shall melt, shall melt a - way, shall
greift die Angst, er - greift, er - greift die Angst, er -
shall melt a - way, shall melt a - way,
er - greift die Angst, er - greift die Angst,
melt a - way, shall melt, shall melt a - way, shall melt a - way, shall
greift die Angst, er - greift, er - greift die Angst, er - greift die Angst, er -
a - way, shall melt, shall melt a - way, shall
die Angst, er - greift, er - greift die Angst, er -
melt a - way, shall melt, shall melt a - way, shall
greift die Angst, er - greift, er - greift die Angst, er -
shall melt a - way, shall melt a - way,
er - greift die Angst, er - greift die Angst,
melt a - way, shall melt, shall melt a - way, shall melt a - way, shall
greift die Angst, er - greift, er - greift die Angst, er - greift die Angst, er -
a - way, shall melt, shall melt a - way, shall
die Angst, er - greift, er - greift die Angst, er -
p

melt a - way, shall
greift die Angst, er -
melt a - way,
greift die Angst,
all th'in - ha - bitants of
all die Ein - ge - bornen
Ca - naan shall
Ka - naan's er -
shall
er -
melt a - way,
greift die Angst,
all th'in - ha - bitants of
all die Ein - ge - bornen
Ca - naan
Ka - naan's
melt, shall
greift, er -
melt a - way,
greift die Angst,
all th'in - ha - bitants of
all die Ein - ge - bornen
Ca - naan
Ka - naan's
melt a - way, shall
greift die Angst, er -
melt a - way,
greift die Angst,
all th'in - ha - bitants of
all die Ein - ge - bornen
Ca - naan
Ka - naan's

melt a-way, shall melt a-way, shall melt a-way, shall melt a-way by the
greift die Angst, er-greift die Angst, ergreift die Angst, er-greift die Angst durch die
shall melt a-way, shall melt a-way by the
er-greift die Angst, er-greift die Angst durch die
shall melt a-way, shall melt, shall melt a-way by the
er-greift die Angst, er-greift, er-greift die Angst durch die
shall melt a-way, shall melt, shall melt a-way by the
er-greift die Angst, er-greift, er-greift die Angst durch die
f
mp
ff

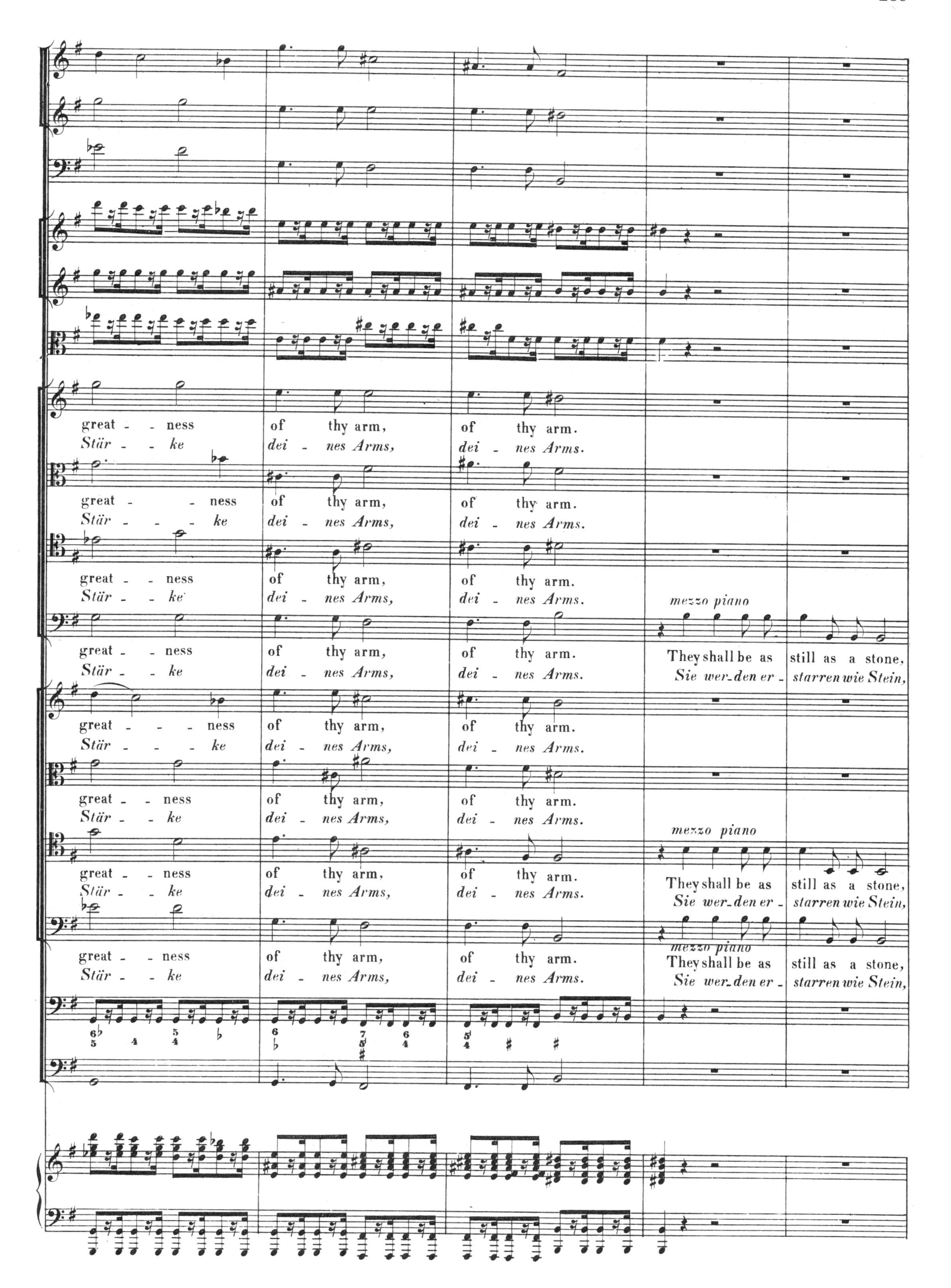

great - ness of thy arm, of thy arm.
Stär - ke dei - nes Arms, dei - nes Arms.
great - - ness of thy arm, of thy arm.
Stär - - ke dei - nes Arms, dei - nes Arms.
great - - ness of thy arm, of thy arm.
Stär - - ke dei - nes Arms, dei - nes Arms.
mezzo piano
great - - ness of thy arm, of thy arm. They shall be as still as a stone,
Stär - - ke dei - nes Arms, dei - nes Arms. Sie wer-den er - starren wie Stein,
great - - - ness of thy arm, of thy arm.
Stär - - - ke dei - nes Arms, dei - nes Arms.
great - - ness of thy arm, of thy arm.
Stär - - ke dei - nes Arms, dei - nes Arms.
mezzo piano
great - - ness of thy arm, of thy arm. They shall be as still as a stone,
Stär - - ke dei - nes Arms, dei - nes Arms. Sie wer-den er - starren wie Stein,
mezzo piano
great - - ness of thy arm, of thy arm. They shall be as still as a stone,
Stär - - ke dei - nes Arms, dei - nes Arms. Sie wer-den er - starren wie Stein,

till thy peo-ple pass
bis vor-ü-ber dein
o-ver, oh Lord,
Volk zieht, o Herr,
mf
cresc.

till thy peo-ple pass o - ver, which thou hast pur - cha - sed,
bis vor-ü-ber dein Volk zieht, das du er - wor - ben hast,
o - ver, oh Lord, which thou hast pur - cha - sed,
Volk zieht, o Herr, das du er - wor - ben hast,
o - ver, oh Lord, which thou hast pur - cha - sed; they shall be as
Volk zieht, o Herr, das du er - wor - ben hast; sie wer - den er -
till thy peo-ple pass o - ver, which thou hast pur - cha - sed; they shall be as
bis vor-ü-ber dein Volk zieht, das du er - - wor - ben hast; sie wer - den er -
till thy peo-ple pass o - ver, which thou hast pur - cha - sed,
bis vor-ü-ber dein Volk zieht, das du er - wor - ben hast,
till thy peo - ple pass o - - - ver, which thou hast pur - cha - sed
bis vor-ü - ber dein Volk zieht, das du er - wor - ben hast
till thy peo - ple pass o - - - ver, which thou hast pur - cha - sed; they shall be as
bis vor - ü - ber dein Volk zieht, das du er - wor - ben hast; sie wer - den er -
till thy peo-ple pass o - ver, which thou hast pur - cha - sed; they shall be as
bis vor-ü-ber dein Volk zieht, das du er - - wor - ben hast; sie wer - den er -
f

till thy peo-ple pass
bis vor-ü-ber dein
o-ver, oh Lord,
Volk zieht, o Herr,
till thy peo-ple pass
bis vor-ü-ber dein
till thy peo-ple pass
bis vor-ü-ber dein
o-ver, oh Lord,
Volk zieht, o Herr,
still as a stone,
star-ren wie Stein,
till thy peo-ple pass
bis vor-ü-ber dein
o-ver, oh Lord,
Volk zieht, o Herr,
still as a stone,
star-ren wie Stein,
till thy peo-ple pass
bis vor-ü-ber dein
till thy peo-ple pass
bis vor-ü-ber dein
o-ver, oh Lord,
Volk zieht, o Herr,
till thy peo-ple pass
bis vor-ü-ber dein
o-ver, oh Lord,
Volk zieht, o Herr,
still as a stone,
star-ren wie Stein,
till thy peo-ple pass
bis vor-ü-ber dein
o-ver, oh Lord,
Volk zieht, o Herr,
still as a stone,
star-ren wie Stein,
till thy peo-ple pass
bis vor-ü-ber dein

o - ver, which thou hast pur - cha - sed, till thy peo-ple pass
Volk zieht, das du er-wor - ben hast, bis vor-ü-ber dein
thy peo - ple which thou hast pur - cha - sed, till thy,
dein Volk zieht, das du er-wor - ben hast, bis vor-
which thou hast pur-cha - sed, till thy peo-ple pass o - ver, oh Lord,
das du er-wor-ben hast, bis vor-ü-ber dein Volk zieht, o Herr,
o - - - ver, which thou hast pur - cha - sed, till thy peo-ple pass o - ver, oh Lord;
Volk zieht, das du er-wor - ben hast, bis vor-ü-ber dein Volk zieht, o Herr;
thy peo - ple which thou hast pur - cha - sed, till thy peo-ple pass
dein Volk zieht, das du er-wor - ben hast, bis vor-ü-ber dein
thy peo - ple which thou hast pur - cha - sed, till thy
dein Volk zieht, das du er-wor - ben hast, bis vor-
which thou hast pur - cha - sed, till thy peo-ple pass o - ver, oh Lord,
das du er-wor - ben hast, bis vor-ü-ber dein Volk zieht, o Herr,
o - - - ver. which thou hast pur - cha - sed, till thy peo-ple pass o - ver, oh Lord;
Volk zieht, das du er-wor - ben hast, bis vor-ü-ber dein Volk zieht, o Herr;
f
fp

o - ver, oh Lord,
Volk zieht, o Herr,
till thy people pass
bis vor - ü - ber dein
o - - - - - - ver,
Volk zieht,
which thou hast pur - - cha -
das du er - wor - - ben
people pass o - ver, oh
ü - ber dein Volk zieht, o
Lord,
Herr,
till thy people pass
bis vor - ü - ber dein
o - - - ver, oh
Volk zieht, o
till thy people pass
bis vor - ü - ber dein
o - - - ver, oh
Volk zieht, o
they shall be as
sie wer - den er -
still as a
star - - ren wie
stone,
Stein,
as a
wie ein
o - ver, oh Lord,
Volk zieht, o Herr,
till thy people pass
bis vor - ü - ber dein
o - - - - - - ver
Volk zieht,
which thou hast pur - - cha -
das du er - wor - - ben
people pass o - ver, oh
ü - ber dein Volk zieht, o
Lord,
Herr,
they shall be as
sie wer - den er -
still as a
star - - ren wie
stone,
Stein,
as a
wie ein
7

sed,
hast,
till thy people pass
bis vor-ü-ber dein
o - - ver, oh
Volk zieht, o
Lord,
Herr,
Lord,
Herr,
till thy people pass
bis vor-ü-ber dein
o - - - ver, oh
Volk zieht, o
Lord,
Herr,
till thy people pass
bis vor-ü-ber dein
o - - - ver, oh
Volk zieht, o
stone,
Stein,
as a
wie ein
stone, till thy people pass
Stein, bis vor-ü-ber dein
sed,
hast,
till thy people pass
bis vor-ü-ber dein
o - - ver, oh
Volk zieht, o
Lord,
Herr,
till thy people pass
bis vor-ü-ber dein
o - ver, oh Lord,
Volk zieht, o Herr,
till thy people pass
bis vor-ü-ber dein
o - ver, oh Lord,
Volk zieht, o Herr,
stone,
Stein,
as a
wie ein
stone, till thy people pass
Stein, bis vor-ü-ber dein
sf

Lord, oh
Herr, o
Lord,
Herr,
till thy peo-ple pass
bis vor-ü-ber dein
Lord, oh
Herr, o
Lord,
Herr,
o - ver, oh Lord, oh
Volk zieht, o Herr, o
Lord, till thy people pass
Herr, bis vor-ü-ber dein
o - ver, oh Lord,
Volk zieht, o Herr,
till thy peo-ple pass
bis vor-ü-ber dein
till thy peo-ple pass
bis vor-ü-ber dein
o - ver, oh Lord,
Volk zieht, o Herr,
till thy peo-ple pass
bis vor-ü-ber dein
o - ver, oh Lord,
Volk zieht, o Herr,
o - ver, oh Lord, oh
Volk zieht, o Herr, o
Lord, till thy peo-ple pass
Herr, bis vor-ü-ber dein
o - ver, oh Lord,
Volk zieht, o Herr,
sf

o - ver, oh Lord,
Volk zieht, o Herr,
thy peo - ple
dein Volk zieht,
which thou hast pur - cha - sed, till thy peo-ple pass
das du er - wor - ben hast, bis vor - ü - ber dein
o - ver, oh Lord,
Volk zieht, o Herr,
thy peo - ple
dein Volk zieht,
which thou hast pur - cha - sed, till thy peo-ple pass
das du er - wor - ben hast, bis vor - ü - ber dein
till thy peo-ple pass
bis vor - ü - ber dein
o - ver
Volk zieht,
which thou hast pur-cha - sed,
das du er - wor - ben hast,
thy peo - ple
dein Volk zieht,
which thou hast pur - cha - sed; they shall be
das du er - wor - ben hast; sie wer - den
o - ver, oh Lord,
Volk zieht, o Herr,
thy peo - ple
dein Volk zieht,
which thou hast pur - cha - sed,
das du er - wor - ben hast,
till thy peo-ple pass
bis vor - ü - ber dein
o - ver
Volk zieht,
which thou hast pur - cha - sed,
das du er - wor - ben hast,
thy peo - ple
dein Volk zieht,
which thou hast pur-cha - sed,
das du er - wor - ben hast,
thy peo - ple
dein Volk zieht,
which thou hast pur - cha - sed; they shall be
das du er - wor - ben hast; sie wer - den
f
fp

o - - ver, oh Lord, till thy people pass o - ver, which
Volk zieht, o Herr, bis vor-ü-ber dein Volk zieht, das
o - - ver, oh Lord, till thy people pass o - - ver, oh Lord, which
Volk zieht, o Herr, bis vor-ü-ber dein Volk zieht, o Herr, das
till thy people pass o - - ver, oh Lord, till thy people pass o - ver, which
bis vor-ü-ber dein Volk zieht, o Herr, bis vor-ü-ber dein Volk zieht, das
still, till thy people pass o - - ver, oh Lord,
starr, bis vor-ü-ber dein Volk zieht, o Herr,
till thy people pass o - - ver, oh Lord, which
bis vor-ü-ber dein Volk zieht, o Herr, das
till thy peo-ple pass o - - ver, which
bis vor-ü - ber dein Volk zieht, das
till thy peo-ple pass o - - ver, which
bis vor-ü - ber dein Volk zieht, das
still, till thy people pass o - - ver, oh Lord, which
starr, bis vor-ü-ber dein Volk zieht, o Herr, das
sf
f

thou hast pur - cha - sed, till thy peo-ple pass o - ver, which thou hast pur - cha - sed.
du er - wor - ben hast, bis vor - ü - ber dein Volk zieht, das du er - wor - ben hast.
thou hast pur - cha - sed, which thou hast pur - cha - sed.
du er - wor - ben hast, das du er - wor - ben hast.
thou hast pur-cha - sed, which thou hast pur - cha - sed.
du er - wor-ben hast, das du er - wor - ben hast.
thou hast pur - cha - sed, which thou hast pur - cha - sed.
du er - wor - ben hast, das du er - wor - ben hast.
thou hast pur - cha - sed, till thy peo-ple pass o - ver, which thou hast pur - cha - sed.
du er - wor - ben hast, bis vor - ü - ber dein Volk zieht, das du er - wor - ben hast.
thou hast pur - cha - sed, which thou hast pur - cha - sed.
du er - wor - ben hast, das du er - wor - ben hast.
thou hast pur - cha - sed, which thou hast pur - cha - sed.
du er - wor - ben hast, das du er - wor - ben hast.
thou hast pur - cha - sed, which thou hast pur - cha - sed.
du er - wor - ben hast, das du er - wor - ben hast.

Largo, e mezzo piano.
Violino I.
Violino II.
ALTO.
Bassi.
Largo, e mezzo piano.
Pianoforte.
Thou shalt bring them in,
Brin - ge sie hin- ein,
thou shalt bring them in, and plant them in the moun -
brin - ge sie hin- ein, und pflan - ze sie auf den Ber -

tain of thine in - he - ritance, in the place, oh Lord, which thou hast
gen in dei - nem Erb - theil, an den Ort, o Herr, den du er -
made, which thou hast made for thee to dwell in, for thee to dwell in,
höh't, den du er - höh't zu dei - ner Woh - nung, zu dei - ner Woh - nung,
to dwell in,
zur Woh - nung

p
p
in the sanc tu a - ry, oh Lord,
und zu dei - nem Hei - lig- thum, o Herr,
p
6
6
6 4
5 3
p
6
p dolce
mp
tr
tr
which thy hands have e sta - - - - - - - - blish
das dei-ne Hand hat be rei - - - - - - - - -
6
6 4
5 3
p
ed,
tet,
in the sanc - - - - tu a -
und zu dei - - - nem Hei -
mf
p

ry,
which thy
hands have e
sta
lig
thum,
das dei_ne
Hand hat be_
rei
blish_ed,
which thy
hands have
e_sta_blish
_ed.
tet,
das dei_ne
Hand hat
be_rei
tet.
a tempo.

CHORUS.
A tempo giusto.
Trombone I.II.
Trombone III.
Tromba I.II.
Timpani.
Oboe I.II.
Fagotti.
Violino I.
Violino II.
Viola.
SOPRANO I.
The
ALTO I.
The Lord shall reign for e - ver and e - - - ver. Der
Der Herr re - - giert auf im - mer und e - - - wig!
TENORE I.
The Lord shall reign for e - ver and e - - - ver. The
Der Herr re - - giert auf im - mer und e - - - wig!
BASSO I.
Der
SOPRANO II.
The
ALTO II.
The Lord shall reign for e - ver and e - - - ver. Der
Der Herr re - - giert auf im - mer und e - - - wig!
TENORE II.
The Lord shall reign for e - ver and e - - - ver. The
Der Herr re - - giert auf im - mer und e - - - wig!
BASSO II.
Der
Tutti Bassi, e Organo.
A tempo giusto.
Pianoforte.
f
ff

Lord shall reign for e - - ver and e - - - - - ver,
Herr re - giert auf im - mer und e - - - - - wig,
Lord shall reign for e - - ver and e - - - - - ver,
Herr re - giert auf im - mer und e - - - - - wig,
Lord shall reign for e - - ver and e - - - - - ver,
Herr re - giert auf im - mer und e - - - - - wig,
Lord shall reign for e - - ver and e - - - - - ver,
Herr re - giert auf im - mer und e - - - - - wig,
tr

the Lord shall reign for e - ver and e - - - ver.
der Herr re - giert auf im - mer und e - - - wig!
the Lord shall reign for e - ver and e - - - ver.
der Herr re - giert auf im - mer und e - - - wig!
the Lord shall reign for e - ver and e - - - ver.
der Herr re - giert auf im - mer und e - - - wig!
the Lord shall reign for e - ver and e - - - ver.
der Herr re - giert auf im - mer und e - - - wig!
6

CHORUS:

The Lord shall reign for ever and ever.

Der Herr regiert auf immer und ewig.

ut supra pag. **254__256.**

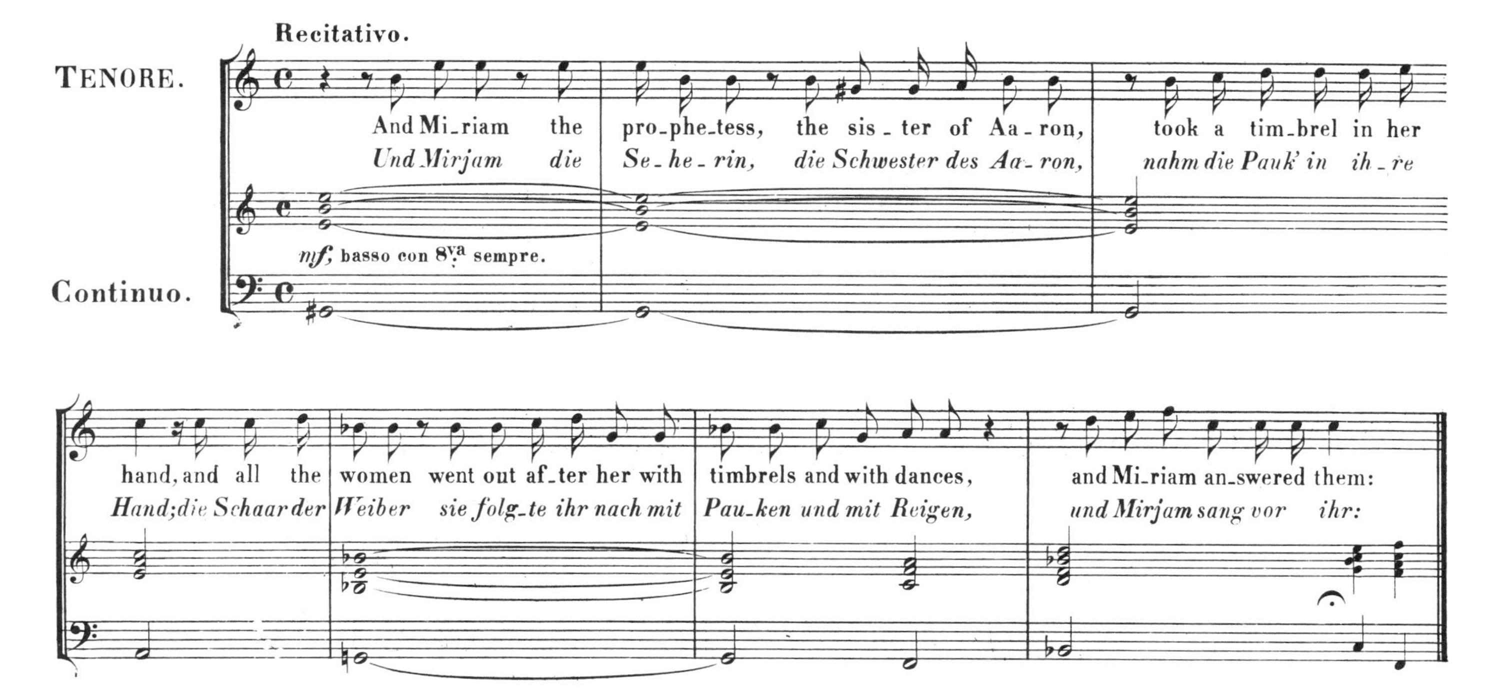

CHORUS.
A tempo giusto.
Trombone I. II.
Trombone III.
Tromba I. II.
Timpani.
Oboe I.
Oboe II.
Fagotti.
Violino I.
Violino II.
Viola.
SOPRANO I.
Solo.
Sing ye to the Lord, for he hath tri - umphed glorious - ly!
Sin - get zu dem Herrn, denn er hat ge - sie - get wun - der - bar!
Tutti.
The Lord shall
ALTO I.
Der Herr re - -
TENORE I.
The Lord shall
BASSO I.
Der Herr re - -
SOPRANO II.
The Lord shall
ALTO II.
Der Herr re - -
TENORE II.
The Lord shall
BASSO II.
Der Herr re - -
Tutti Bassi.
Organo.
A tempo giusto.
Pianoforte.

Solo.
reign for e - - ver and e - - - - - - - - ver.
The horse and his
Das Ross und den
giert auf im - - mer und e - - - - - - - wig!
reign for e - - ver and e - - - - - - - - ver.
giert auf im - - mer und e - - - - - - - wig!
reign for e - - ver and e - - - - - - - - ver.
giert auf im - - mer und e - - - - - - - wig!
reign for e - - ver and e - - - - - - - - ver.
giert auf im - - mer und e - - - - - - - wig!
p

Tutti.
ri_der hath he thrown in_to the sea.
Rei_ter hat er in das Meer ge_stürzt.
The Lord shall reign for
Der Herr re_ _ _giert auf
The Lord shall reign for
Der Herr re_ _ _giert auf
The Lord shall reign for
Der Herr re_ _ _giert auf
The Lord shall reign for
Der Herr re_ _ _giert auf
f

e - - - ver and e - - - - - - - - ver:
im - - mer und e - - - - - - - - wig: for he hath triumphed glo - - - - - - - - -
denn er hat ge-hol-fen wun - - - - - - - - -
e - - ver and e - - - - - - - - ver: for he hath triumphed glo - - -
denn er hat gehol - fen wun - - -
im - - mer und e - - - - - - - - wig:
e - - ver and e - - - - - - - - ver:
im - - mer und e - - - - - - - - wig: for he hath triumphed glo - - - - - - - - -
denn er hat ge-hol-fen wun - - - - - - - - -
e - - ver and e - - - - - - - - ver: for he hath triumphed glo - - -
denn er hat gehol - fen wun - - -
im - - mer und e - - - - - - - - wig:

for he
denn er
hath triumphed glo
hat ge-holfen wun
riously,
derbar,
glo-riously,
wun-derbar,
gloriously,
wunderbar,
glo-riously,
wun-derbar,
for he hath triumphed
denn er hat ge-hol-fen
glo
wun
for he hath triumphed
denn er hat ge-hol-fen
der-bar,
for he
denn er

for he hath triumphed
denn er hat ge_hol_fen
for he
denn er
gloriously, glo - - - riously, glo - - - - riously, glo - - - - - - - riously,
wun_derbar, wun - - - derbar, wun - - - - derbar, wun - - - - - - - derbar,
glo - - riously, glo - - - riously, glo - - - riously, he hath tri_umphed gloriously,
wun - - derbar, wun - - - derbar, wun - - - der_bar, er hat ge_holfen wunderbar,
gloriously, gloriously, gloriously, glo_riously, glo_riously, gloriously, he hath tri_umphed gloriously,
wun_derbar, wun_derbar, wunderbar, wun_derbar, wun_derbar, wunder_bar, er hat ge_holfen wunderbar,
hath triumphed glo - - - riously, gloriously,
hat ge_holfen wun - - - derbar, wunderbar,

glo - riously,
wun - der-bar,
hath triumphed glo - riously,
hat ge-hol-fen wun - der-bar,
the horse and his ri-der
das Ross und den Rei-ter
the horse and his ri-der hath he
das Ross und den Rei-ter hat ge-

I will sing unto the
ich will sin - gen zu dem
I will sing, the horse and his ri-der hath he thrown in-to the
ich will sin-gen, das Ross und den Rei-ter hat ge-stürzt er in das
the horse and his ri-der, the horse and his ri-der hath he thrown in-to the
das Ross und den Rei-ter, das Ross und den Rei-ter hat ge-stürzt er in das
hath he thrown in-to the sea;
hat ge-stürzt er in das Meer,
thrown in-to the sea,
stürzt er in das Meer;

Lord, un - - to the Lord,
Herrn, zu dem Herrn,
sea, in-to the sea,
Meer, ge-stürzt in's Meer,
sea, in-to the sea,
Meer, ge-stürzt in's Meer,
I will sing
ich will sin -
the horse, the horse and his ri - der, the horse and his ri - der
das Ross, das Ross und den Rei-ter, das Ross und den Rei-ter
the horse and his ri - der, the horse and his ri - der, the horse and his ri - der
das Ross und den Rei-ter, das Ross und den Rei-ter, das Ross und den Rei-ter
I will sing
ich will sin -

he
er
hath triumphed glo - riously,
hat ge-hol-fen wun - derbar,
he
er
hath triumphed glo-riously,
hat ge-hol-fen wun-der-bar,
glo-riously,
wun-derbar,
gloriously,
wunderbar,
he hath triumphed
er hat ge-hol-fen
glo-riously,
wun-derbar,
gloriously,
wunderbar,
he hath triumphed
er hat ge-hol-fen
glo - riously,
wun - derbar,
un-to the Lord,
-gen zu dem Herrn,
he
er
hath he thrown in-to the sea,
hat gestürzt er in das Meer,
he hath triumphed
er hat ge-holfen
hath he thrown in-to the sea,
hat gestürzt er in das. Meer,
he hath triumphed
er hat ge-holfen
un-to the Lord,
-gen zu dem Herrn,
he
er
6 7

the horse and his ri - der
das Ross und den Rei - ter
the horse and his ri - der hath he
das Ross und den Rei - ter hat ge -
the horse and his ri - der
das Ross und den Rei - ter
the horse and his ri - der hath he
das Ross und den Rei - ter hat ge -
hath triumphed glo - riously, he hath tri - umphed gloriously,
hat ge - hol - fen wun - der - bar, er hat ge - hol - fen wun - derbar,
glo - riously;
wun - der - bar;
glo - riously;
wun - der - bar;
hath triumphed glo - riously,
hat ge - hol - fen wun - der - bar,

hath he thrown in-to the sea;
hat ge-stürzt er in das Meer;
thrown in - to the sea.
stürzt er in das Meer,
hath he thrown in-to the sea,
hat ge-stürzt er in das Meer,
thrown in - to the sea;
stürzt er in das Meer;
the horse and his ri-der, the horse and his ri-der hath he thrown in-to the
das Ross und den Rei-ter, das Ross und den Rei-ter hat ge-stürzt er in das
I will sing un-to the
ich will sin-gen zu dem
I will sing un-to the
ich will sin-gen zu dem
the horse and his ri-der, the horse and his ri-der hath he thrown in-to the
das Ross und den Rei-ter, das Ross und den Rei-ter hat ge-stürzt er in das

I will sing
ich will sin
the horse and his ri-der, the horse and his ri-der, the horse and his ri-der hath
das Ross und den Rei-ter, das Ross und den Rei-ter, das Ross und den Rei-ter hat
the horse and his ri-der, the horse and his ri-der
das Ross und den Rei-ter, das Ross und den Rei-ter
I will sing
ich will sin
sea, into the sea,
Meer, ge-stürzt ins Meer,
Lord, un-to the Lord,
Her-ren, zu dem Herrn,
Lord, un-to the Lord,
Her-ren, zu dem Herrn,
sea, in-to the sea,
Meer, ge-stürzt ins Meer,

un - to the Lord, un - to the Lord,
- gen zu dem Her - ren, zu dem Herrn,
he
er
he thrown in - to the sea, hath he thrown in - to the sea,
er gestürzt in das Meer, hat ge - stürzt er in das Meer,
hath he thrown in - to the sea, in - to the sea,
hat ge - stürzt er in das Meer, ge - stürzt in's Meer,
he
er
un - to the Lord,
- gen zu dem Herrn,
he hath triumphed glo -
er hat ge - holfen wun -
he hath triumphed glo - riously, glo - riously,
er hat ge - holfen wun - derbar, wun - der - bar,
he hath triumphed glo - riously, glo - riously,
er hat ge - holfen wun - derbar, wun - der - bar,
he hath triumphed glo -
er hat ge - holfen wun -

hath triumphed glo - - - riously, the horse and his ri-der, the horse
hat ge-holfen wun - - - derbar,
he hath triumphed glo-riously, glo-riously, gloriously, das Ross und den Reiter, das Ross
er hat ge-hol-fen wun-derbar, wun-derbar, wunderbar,
hath triumphed glo-riously, glo-riously, gloriously, the horse and his ri-der, the horse
hat ge-holfen wun-derbar, wun-derbar, wunderbar,
he hath triumphed glo - - - riously, das Ross und den Reiter, das Ross
er hat ge-hol-fen wun - - - derbar,
- riously, the horse and his ri-der, the horse and his
- derbar,
gloriously, das Ross und den Reiter, das Ross und den
wunderbar,
gloriously, the horse and his ri-der, the horse and his
wunderbar,
- riously, das Ross und den Reiter, das Ross und den
- derbar,

and his ri_der hath he thrown in_to the sea, the horse and his ri_der, the
und den Reiter hat gestürzt er in das Meer, das Ross und den Reiter, das
and his ri_der hath he thrown in_to the sea, the horse and his ri_der, the
und den Reiter hat gestürzt er in das Meer, das Ross und den Reiter, das
ri_der hath he thrown, hath he thrown in_to the sea, the horse and his ri_der, the
Rei_ter hat gestürzt, hat ge_ stürzt er in das Meer, das Ross und den Reiter, das
ri_der hath he thrown, hath he thrown in_to the sea, the horse and his ri_der, the
Rei_ter hat gestürzt, hat ge_ stürzt er in das Meer, das Ross und den Reiter, das
ff

horse and his ri-der, the horse and his ri-der, the horse and his ri-der hath he thrown in-to the sea, the
Ross und den Rei-ter, das Ross und den Reiter, das Ross und den Reiter hat er ge-stürzt in das Meer, das
horse and his ri-der, the horse and his ri-der, the horse and his ri-der hath he thrown in-to the sea, the
Ross und den Rei-ter, das Ross und den Reiter, das Ross und den Reiter hat er ge-stürzt in das Meer, das
horse and his ri-der, the horse and his ri-der, the horse and his ri-der hath he thrown in-to the sea, the
Ross und den Rei-ter, das Ross und den Reiter, das Ross und den Reiter hat er ge-stürzt in das Meer, das
horse and his ri-der, the horse and his ri-der, the horse and his ri-der hath he thrown in-to the sea, the
Ross und den Rei-ter, das Ross und den Reiter, das Ross und den Reiter hat er ge-stürzt in das Meer, das

horse and his ri_der, the horse and his ri_der hath
he thrown in_to the sea;
Ross und den Rei_ter, das Ross und den Rei_ter hat
er ge_stürzt in das Meer;
horse and his ri_der, the horse and his ri_der hath
he thrown in_to the sea;
Ross und den Rei_ter, das Ross und den Rei_ter hat
er ge_stürzt in das Meer;
I
will
ich
will
horse and his ri_der, the horse and his ri_der hath
he thrown in_to the sea;
Ross und den Rei_ter, das Ross und den Rei_ter hat
er ge_stürzt in das Meer;
horse and his ri_der, the horse and his ri_der hath
he thrown in_to the sea;
Ross und den Rei_ter, das Ross und den Rei_ter hat
er ge_stürzt in das Meer;
I
will
ich
will
mf

I will sing unto the Lord, for he
ich will singen zu dem Herrn, denn er
I will sing unto the Lord, for he hath triumphed
ich will singen zu dem Herrn, denn er hat geholfen
I will sing unto the Lord,
ich will singen zu dem Herrn,
sing unto the Lord, for he
singen zu dem Herrn, denn er
I will sing unto the Lord, for he
ich will singen zu dem Herrn, denn er
I will sing unto the Lord, for he hath triumphed
ich will singen zu dem Herrn, denn er hat geholfen
I will sing unto the Lord,
ich will singen zu dem Herrn,
sing unto the Lord, for he
singen zu dem Herrn, denn er

hath triumphed glo - riously, he hath triumphed glo - riously, the
hat ge-hol-fen wun - der-bar,
glo - riously, glo - riously, glo - riously, er
wun - der-bar, wun - der-bar, wun - der-bar, hat ge-hol-fen wun - der-bar, das
for he hath tri - umphed glo-rious - ly, glo - riously, he hath triumphed glo - riously, the
denn er hat ge - hol-fen wun-der - bar, wun - der-bar,
hath triumphed glo - riously, er
hat ge-hol-fen wun - der-bar, hat ge-hol-fen wun - der-bar, das
ff

horse and his ri-der hath he thrown in-to the sea, the horse and his ri-der, the horse and his ri-der hath
Ross und den Reiter hat er ge-stürzt in das Meer, das Ross und den Rei-ter, das Ross und den Rei-ter hat
horse and his ri-der hath he thrown in-to the sea, the horse and his ri-der, the horse and his ri-der hath
Ross und den Reiter hat er ge-stürzt in das Meer, das Ross und den Rei-ter, das Ross und den Rei-ter hat
horse and his ri-der hath he thrown in-to the sea, the horse and his ri-der, the horse and his ri-der hath
Ross und den Reiter hat er ge-stürzt in das Meer, das Ross und den Rei-ter, das Ross und den Rei-ter hat
horse and his ri-der hath he thrown in-to the sea, the horse and his ri-der, the horse and his ri-der hath
Ross und den Reiter hat er ge-stürzt in das Meer, das Ross und den Rei-ter, das Ross und den Rei-ter hat

END OF EDITION